BIG ENGLISH 2 PLUS

Mario Herrera • Christopher Sol Cruz

PUPIL'S BOOK

Contents

CLIL/Culture	Values	Phonics	I can...
Maths: Sums numbers 11–100, plus, minus, equals 10 minus 6 equals.../5 plus 5 equals... **Around the World: Classes** in a forest/garden, in the mountains, on a boat	**Take turns.** May I use the computer now? Yes! Let's take turns.	**th** that, the, then, this bath, both, Maths, mouth, thin, think, with	...talk about what people are doing in the classroom. ...count to 100. ...talk about taking turns.
Science: Bones and muscles bone, exercise, jump, kick, move, muscle, strong, throw, weak We throw with our hands. When we jump, we use ... muscles. **Around the World: Games**	**Play safely.** safe, seesaw, skateboard, slide, swing I want to play on the slide. Always slide with your feet in front of you.	**ng, nk** bang, king, ring, sing, wing bank, ink, pink, sink, thank	...say what people like doing. ...talk about how my body works. ...talk about playing safely.
History: Old and new things burn, museum, new, oil, old, screen, wheel This is an old phone. / This phone is old. **Around the World: Household objects** clay, comfortable, dry, electricity, fuel, hammock, household, solar, wet	**Be tidy.** sink, toy box, washing machine	**oo** boot, cool, food, moon, room, zoo book, cook, foot, good, look	...say where things are. ...talk about possessions. ...talk about new and old objects.
Geography: Transport around the world boat, canal, fast, ground, safe, slow, underground In Bangkok, many students go to school by boat. **Around the World: Taxis** design, famous, long time ago, sign	**Cross the road safely.** first, left, pedestrian crossing, right, road, wait	**ai, oa** nail, rain, tail, train, wait boat, coat, oak, road, soap	...say what I want and talk about money. ...describe where places are in town. ...talk about different kinds of transport.
Social Science: Goods and services carpenter, entertain, farmer, hairdresser, nurse, produce, provide, take care of, waiter A nurse helps ill people. **Around the World: Jobs** park ranger, protect, rodeo rider, scuba diver	**Study hard and set goals.** Art, Maths, Music, Science	**ar, er, or** arm, art, car, cart letter, singer, teacher born, corn, for	...talk about jobs. ...say what I want to be and why. ...talk about studying hard and setting goals.
History: Telling the time burn, candle, cup, fall, height, hourglass, sand, shadow, sundial We use clocks to tell the time. **Around the World: Routines** after/before school, break, tired	**Be on time.** I get my backpack ready the night before school. I get up early on school days. I get dressed quickly and eat breakfast. I always get to school on time.	**ch, tch, sh** chin, chop, lunch, rich match, watch, witch dish, fish, ship, shop	...talk about times and daily activities. ...ask questions. ...talk about different ways of telling time.
Science: Healthy and unhealthy snacks diabetes, disease, fat, healthy, heart, label, salt, sugar, too much, unhealthy **Around the World: Fruit** avocado, chocolate, fabric, kiwi, leaves, pineapple, popular, round, square, tropical, watermelon	**Choose healthy foods.** apple, biscuit, carrots, crisps No crisps for me, thanks. Just one biscuit, please.	**ee, ie** bee, cheese, feet, see, sheep cried, flies, lie, pie, tie	...talk about food. ...talk about healthy and unhealthy food. ...say where fruit comes from.
Science: Animal habitats cover, desert, fox, jungle, lizard, ocean, raccoon, seal, whale Lizards live in deserts. **Around the World: Outside my window** gum tree, interesting, koala, llama, snowball, website, wonderful	**Appreciate animals.** amazing, beautiful, clever, strong	**ou, ow** group, route, soup, toucan, you clown, cow, down, owl, town	...describe animals. ...talk about where animals live. ...talk about appreciating animals.
Geography: Seasonal festivals celebration, confetti, hang, pole, wish In England, people celebrate May Day. May Day is in spring. **Around the World: New Year's Eve** chime, coal, fireworks, good luck, grapes, midnight, noodle soup, ring	**Be active all year.** rake leaves, ride bikes, skate on ice, swim	**Alphabet**	...talk about what I do each month. ...talk about the weather. ...talk about seasonal holidays.

In My Classroom

1 🎧² Listen, look and say.

1 colouring

2 counting

3 cutting

4 gluing

5 listening

6 watching a DVD

7 using the computer

8 writing

9 playing a game

2 🎧³ Listen, find and say. **3** Play a game.

4 Listen and sing. Then look at 1 and find.

Here's My Classroom!

Look! Here's my classroom.
And here are my friends!
Peter, Sarah and Timothy,
Penny, Jack and Jen!

Peter is cutting paper.
Penny is writing her name.
Sarah is listening to a story
And Jack is playing a game.

Timothy is counting.
Jen is gluing.
We have fun and learn a lot.
What are your friends doing?

5 Listen and find in 1. Then say.

6 Look at 1. Ask and answer.

What's she doing?

She's colouring.

**THINK BIG What can we write?
What can we count?**

7 Listen and read. How many Marias are there?

8 Look at the story. Then match.

1 She's cutting paper.

2 She's gluing pictures.

3 She's using the computer.

4 She's writing on the board.

a

b

THINK BIG Are there any girls called Maria in your class? How many?
How many children are there with the same name? What are the names?

9 Listen. Help Jamie and Jenny make sentences.

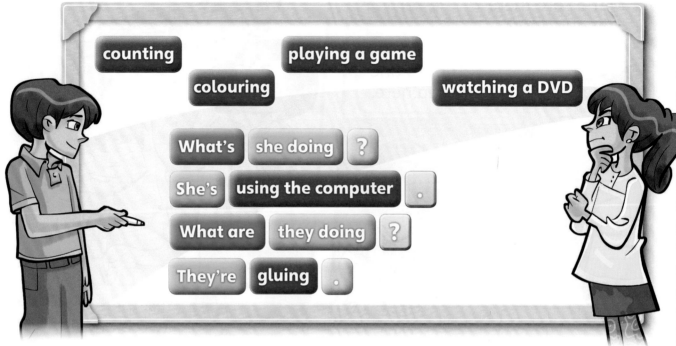

counting

playing a game

colouring

watching a DVD

What's | she doing | ?

She's | using the computer | .

What are | they doing | ?

They're | gluing | .

10 Look and write.

1 What's he _____?

He's _____ his name.

2 What's she _____?

_____ a picture.

3 _____ they _____?

_____ to a story.

4 _____?

_____ paper.

12

11 Listen and stick. Then say.

12 Look at 11. Ask and answer. Use How many.

How many computers are there?

There are two computers.

13 Draw and write. Use There's or There are.

_____

_____

Do the Maths. Then listen and check.

1 Four plus three equals _____.

2 Eight minus two equals _____.

3 One plus nine equals _____.

> **CONTENT WORDS**
>
> plus +
>
> minus –
>
> equals =

 Look, listen and read. Then match and write a–e.

> **CONTENT WORDS**
>
> eleven 11   twelve 12   thirteen 13   fourteen 14   fifteen 15   sixteen 16
> seventeen 17   eighteen 18   nineteen 19   twenty 20   thirty 30   forty 40
> fifty 50   sixty 60   seventy 70   eighty 80   ninety 90   one hundred 100

Maths Homework   Katie Timms

1 There are eleven girls in the class and nineteen boys. There are __thirty__ children in the class. ☐

2 There are fourteen chairs in Classroom 1. The children move thirteen of them to Classroom 2. Now there are __fifty__ chairs in Classroom 1. ☐

3 The children have got fifteen cakes. They eat four. Now they've got __twelve__ cakes. ☐

4 There are eighteen pictures on the paper. Lucy cuts out sixteen pictures. Now there are __two__ pictures on the paper. ☐

5 There are one hundred children in the playground. Forty go into their classrooms. Now there are __seventy__ children in the playground. ☐

a $14 - 13 = 50$ ✗   b $100 - 40 = 70$ ✗

c $11 + 19 = 30$ ✓   d $15 - 4 = 12$ ✗

e $18 - 16 = 2$ ✓

THINK BIG **When do adults use Maths?**

16 **Listen and circle. Then ask and answer.**

1 17 / **70**

2 **59** / 95

3 **69** / 89

4 **31** / 33

5 **47** / **27**

6 **23** / 22

What's this?

Sixty-nine!

 **17** **Count and write, then listen. Then say and answer.**

1 30 + 40 = ☐

2 20 - 2 = ☐

3 60 - 10 = ☐

4 11 + 1 = ☐

5 80 + 4 = ☐

6 19 - 6 = ☐

7 17 - 3 = ☐

8 95 + 5 = ☐

Thirty plus forty equals…

Seventy!

PROJECT

18 **Make a Maths poster. Then present it to the class.**

+

Here are twelve pens. Here are three pens. There are fifteen pens. Twelve plus three equals fifteen.

12   +   3   =   15
Twelve plus three equals fifteen.

19 **Listen and read. Then say.**

Mrs Green:	It's hot in the classroom. Open the window, please, Lucy.
Lucy:	OK.
Mrs Green:	Don't stand on the table. There's a computer on it! Be careful!
Lucy:	Can I stand on the computer?
Mrs Green:	Don't be silly! Stand on the chair, open the window and then sit down. And be quick, please, Lucy.

 20 **Read. Then circle Don't in 19.**

Stand on the chair. **Be** careful.	**Don't stand** on the table. **Don't be** silly.

Stand on the chair. ✔
You stand on the chair. ✘

Be careful! ✔
Are careful! ✘

Don't (= Do not) stand on the table. ✔
Don't be silly. ✔

 21 **Read and circle.**

Class Rules

1 **Listen / Don't listen** to the teacher.

2 **Talk / Don't talk** when the teacher is talking.

3 **Be / Don't be** careful when you're cutting paper.

4 **Eat / Don't eat** food in the classroom.

22 **Put the words in order. Then say.**

1 quick. Be

2 picture. Colour the

3 use Don't computer. the

4 a Play game.

23 **Look and write.**

1 write ✓   throw ✗
_____ on the paper,
please. _____ it.

2 talk ✗   listen ✓
_____ to your friend.
_____ to the teacher.

3 be ✗   dry ✓
_____ _____ sad.
_____ your eyes.

4 wake up ✓   be ✗
_____ _____, Jenny!
_____ _____ late!

Classes, but Not in a Classroom!

Are classes always in classrooms?   No, they aren't!

These pupils live in the mountains in France. They're having a P.E. class. It's very cold but they're having fun. They love skiing.

These pupils in Turkey aren't in their classroom today. They're in a forest. They're studying trees and animals.

24 **Look at the pictures. Where are the children?**

in a forest   in a garden   in the mountains   on a boat

25 **Listen and read. Then match and write a–d.**

They're doing/studying: **1** P.E. ☐   **2** Science ☐

3 animals ☐   **4** English ☐

26 **Look at 25. Read and circle.**

1 It's **hot** / **cold** in the mountains in France.

2 The pupils in France are **skiing** / **climbing**.

3 There **is** / **isn't** a garden at the school in the United States.

4 The boat school is **always** / **sometimes** open.

These pupils in the United States are having a Science class in the school garden. They're growing plants and flowers.

These pupils are studying English in a classroom in Bangladesh. Their school is a boat! Bangladesh is a wet country. Sometimes schools close, but this school is always open.

27 **Talk about your classroom with a friend.**

Our classroom is in Turkey. There are twenty desks and chairs.

We've got a big whiteboard and six new computers.

THINK BIG **Have you got classes outside the classroom? Where do you go? What do you study?**

28 Listen and look. Number in order.

a

b

c

☐   ☐   ☐

29 Take turns. Ask and answer. Do the actions.

May I use the computer now?

Yes! Let's take turns.

THINK BIG Is it good to take turns? Why?

22
30 **Listen, look and repeat.**

1 th   **2** th

23
31 **Listen and find. Then say.**

bath   **thin**

this   **that**

24
32 **Listen and blend the sounds.**

1 th-e   the   **2** th-e-n   then

3 b-o-th   both   **4** w-i-th   with

5 p-a-th   path   **6** M-a-th-s   Maths

25
33 **Underline th and th. Then listen and chant.**

There are three crocodiles
In the bath.
They've got thin mouths
But big teeth!
Look out! Look out!

Listen and find. Say Picture 1 or Picture 2. Then ask and answer.

Picture 1

Picture 2

In Picture 1, what are they doing?

In Picture 1, they're playing a game.

35 Look and write rules.

1 _____ to the teacher. ✓

2 _____ your name on your notebook. ✓

3 _____ _____ to music. ✗

4 _____ _____ DVDs. ✗

36 Count and write. Use There's or There are.

1 _____

_____ rulers.

2 _____

_____ a rubber.

3 _____

_____ marker pens.

I Can

- ☐ talk about what people are doing in the classroom.
- ☐ count to 100.
- ☐ talk about taking turns.

My Games

28

1 Listen, look and say.

1 flying kites

2 playing volleyball

3 playing tennis

4 climbing trees

5 doing gymnastics

7 skateboarding

6 ice skating

8 riding my bike

29

2 Listen, find and say.   **3** Play a game.

4 Listen and sing. Then look at 1 and find.

Come On and Play

We're playing in the playground.
There are a lot of games to play.
Football, tennis and volleyball.
What do you want to play today?

Paul likes playing on the swings.
Emma likes running and climbing.
We all love riding our bikes.
Tell us! What do you like doing?

We're playing in the playground.
It's always so much fun.
Come on and play with us.
We play with everyone!

5 Listen and ✔.

a
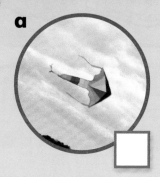

b

c
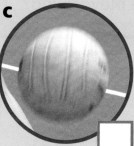

d

6 Look at 1. Ask and answer.

I like playing volleyball.

Number 2.

THINK BIG What games can children play in the playground?
What games can children play in the classroom?

34

7 **Listen and read. What does Jenny like doing?**

8 Look at the story. Then circle.

1  likes **playing football / riding his bike**.

2 loves **playing tennis / skateboarding**.

3  likes **playing volleyball / flying kites**.

 THINK BIG What do you like playing in the playground?
What team games do you know?
Do you like playing in a team? Why?

35

9 Listen. Help Jamie and Jenny make sentences.

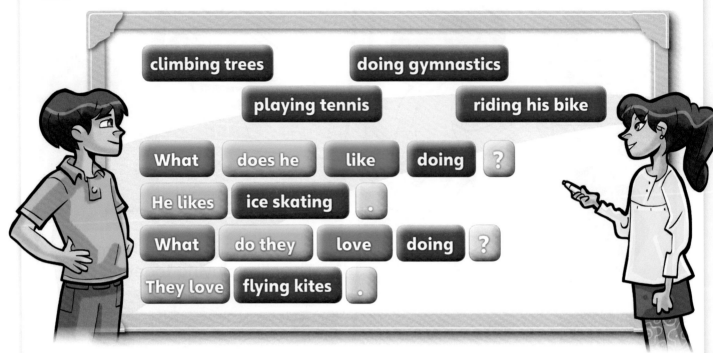

| climbing trees | | doing gymnastics |

| playing tennis | | riding his bike |

What | does he | like | doing | ?

He likes | ice skating | .

What | do they | love | doing | ?

They love | flying kites | .

10 Look and write. Use like or love.

1 What _____ she like doing?
She likes _____.

2 What _____ they love _____?
They _____.

3 _____ you _____?
I _____.

4 _____?
_____.

37
11 Listen and stick. Then say.

12 Look at 11. Ask and answer.

What do they love doing?

They love flying kites.

13 Write and draw.

I love _____

_____

_____

_____.

Look. Circle the body words. How many are they?

| bones | feet | fingers | help | milk | muscles |

38

15 **Look, listen and read. Then circle.**

CONTENT WORDS

bone   exercise   jump   kick   move   muscle   strong   throw   weak

Bones and Muscles

a Playing is fun. Our bones and muscles help us play. Our bodies move when our muscles pull our bones into different positions.

b Our hands have got lots of bones. There are **1 27 / 70** bones in one hand. When we throw a ball with our hands, we use **2 43 / 34** muscles.

c Our feet have got lots of bones, too. There are **3 20 / 26** bones in one foot. When we kick a ball with our foot, we use **4 13 / 30** muscles. When we jump, we use more than **5 17 / 70** muscles.

d When we exercise every day, we use our muscles and they grow strong. But when we don't exercise, they grow weak. Milk, yoghurt and cheese help make our bones strong. We need to take good care of our bones and muscles.

THINK BIG **Which activities make our muscles strong?**
dancing   using a computer   watching DVDs
playing tennis   climbing trees

16 **Look at 15. Read and match.**

1 Bones and muscles   **a** make our bones strong.

2 Our hands   **b** makes our muscles strong.

3 When we throw a ball, we   **c** help us play.

4 When we jump, we   **d** use more than 70 muscles.

5 Exercise   **e** use our hands.

6 Milk and cheese   **f** have got lots of bones.

17 **Look, choose and say.**

| drink milk   eat yoghurt and cheese   exercise |

| bones   muscles   strong   weak |

I exercise every day.

You've got strong muscles.

I don't drink milk.

You've got weak bones.

PROJECT

18 **Make a Body poster about an activity. Then present it to the class.**

Bones and Muscles in Volleyball

I love volleyball.

There are three bones in an arm and 27 bones in a hand.

In volleyball, we hit the ball with our hands and arms.

When we jump, we use more than 70 muscles.

We hit the ball with our hands and arms.

19 **Listen and read. Then say.**

Anna: Does your sister like playing sports?

Ben: She doesn't like playing football or basketball but she loves skateboarding.

Anna: Me, too! It's my favourite sport.

Ben: What about your brothers? What sports do they like?

Anna: They like volleyball and tennis and they love swimming. But they don't like swimming in the sea.

Ben: Me neither! It's very cold.

20 **Read. Then circle don't and doesn't in 19.**

She loves skateboarding. **They love** swimming.	**Me, too!**
She doesn't like playing football. **They don't like** swimming in the sea.	**Me neither!**

I/you/we/they like playing. ✔
He/She/It likes playing. ✔

I/You/We/They don't like ice skating. ✔
He/She/It doesn't like ice skating. ✔

21 **Read and circle.**

1 I love climbing trees.   **Me, too. / Me neither.**

2 My dad doesn't like ice skating.   **Me, too. / Me neither.**

3 My sister hasn't got a skateboard.   **Me, too. / Me neither.**

4 My parents like riding bikes.   **Me, too. / Me neither.**

22 **Look and say.**

1 They (like ✗) playing hopscotch.
2 He (love ✓) playing on the slide.
3 She (have got ✗) a bike.
4 He always (drink ✓) milk for healthy bones.

23 **Write.**

| doesn't | don't | like | loves | neither | too |

A: I love dogs.

B: Me, ¹_____!

A: My dog's name is Billy and he's very funny. He doesn't
²_____ eating bones and he ³_____ like
catching balls but he ⁴_____ skateboarding. I don't
understand it!

B: Me ⁵_____ but my dogs are funny, too. They
⁶_____ like running but they love riding my
mum's bike!

24 **Work with a friend. Look and say.**

Do you like...	Jim and Mehmet	Sarah	Alex
flying kites?	✓	✗	✗
doing gymnastics?	✓	✓	✗
singing?	✗	✗	✓

Jim and Mehmet like flying kites.

Me, too!

Games You Play

1   I like playing jacks. I play on my own but you can play with friends, too. You need a small ball and ten jacks. You throw the ball, then you pick up the jacks before you catch the ball again.

Elena, Guatemala

jack

25 **Look at the pictures. Which games do you know? Who do you play with?**

26 **Listen and read. Then write Elena, Arnav or John.**

1 _____ plays with stones.

2 _____ catches a ball.

3 _____ hits something.

27 **Look at 26. Read and match.**

Name	Game	You need	You
Elena	mancala	marbles	hit
Arnav	jacks	jacks and a ball	move and take
John	marbles	stones and a board	throw, pick up and catch

2   Children in my city like playing marbles after school. Lots of people can play this game together. You hit a marble with your finger. When I win my friends' marbles, I'm very happy.

Arnav, India

board

stone

3   My friends and I like playing mancala. It's a game for two people. You need a board and some stones. You move the stones around the board. It's good when you catch your friend's stones.

John, Ghana

marble

28 **Complete the chart about a game you like. Then ask and answer.**

What's the game?	
What do you need?	
What do you do?	

What's the game?   Hopscotch.

THINK BIG **Which games do you like playing? What do you need for your games?**

43

29 Listen and number.

a

b

c

d

skateboard   swing   seesaw   slide

 44

30 Listen and write. Then say.

| feet | hands | knee | leg |

A

1 I want to play on the slide.

2 I want to play on the swing.

3 I want to play on the seesaw.

4 I want to skateboard.

B

Always slide with your _____ in front of you.

Always sit down and hold on with both _____.

Always put one _____ on each side.

Always wear a helmet and _____ pads.

> I want to play on the slide.

> Always slide with your feet in front of you.

THINK BIG Do you play safely? How?

45
 31 Listen, look and repeat.

1 ng   **2** nk

46
 32 Listen and find. Then say.

ring

bang

pink

ink

47
 33 Listen and blend the sounds.

1 k-i-ng   king   **2** w-i-ng   wing

3 th-a-nk   thank   **4** s-i-ng   sing

5 b-a-nk   bank   **6** s-i-nk   sink

48
 34 Underline ng and nk. Then listen and chant.

Sing a song about a king.
Thank you! Thank you!
He's got a big, pink ring
And big, blue wings.
Thank you! Thank you!

35 **Work in groups. Play the Memory game.**

Pupil 1:
What do you like doing in the playground? Say.

Pupil 2:
Talk about Pupil 1. What does she like doing? Then say and act out what you like doing.

I like playing volleyball.

Susan likes playing volleyball. I like riding my bike.

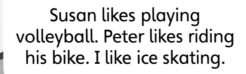

Susan likes playing volleyball. Peter likes riding his bike. I like ice skating.

Pupil 3:
Talk about Pupils 1 and 2. Then say and act out what you like doing.

Play with your group. Can you remember what everyone likes doing?

36 **Look and write. Use like or love.**

1 _____
flying kites.

2 _____
playing tennis.

3 _____
playing football.

4 _____
ice skating.

37 **Write.**

1 A: I like volleyball.   **B:** Me, _____!

2 A: I don't like milk.   **B:** Me _____.

38 **Read and circle.**

1 When we throw, we use our **feet / hands**.

2 When we jump, we use our **arms / legs**.

3 When we kick, we use our **feet / fingers**.

4 When we dance, we use our **nose / toes**.

I Can

☐ **say what people like doing.**

☐ **talk about how my body works.**

☐ **talk about playing safely.**

In My House

living room

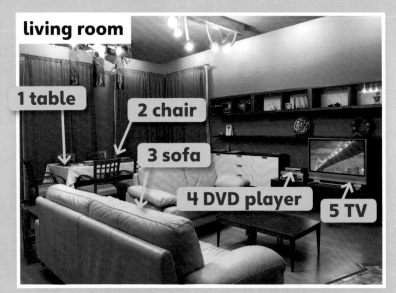

1 table
2 chair
3 sofa
4 DVD player
5 TV

bathroom

6 bath

kitchen

7 fridge
8 sink
9 cooker

bedroom

10 bed
11 dressing table
12 lamp
13 cupboard

4 Listen and sing. Then look at 1 and find.

Where Are My Keys?

Where are my keys, Mum?
Your keys are on the chair.
The chair? Which chair?
There are chairs everywhere!

There's a chair in the living room
And one in the bedroom, too.
There are chairs in the dining room.
I don't know which chair. Do you?

Your keys are where you left them.
Put on your glasses and see.
They're on the chair behind you.
My keys are there! Silly me!

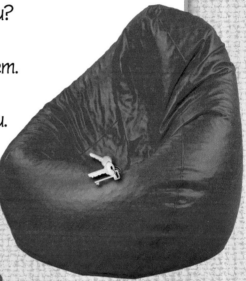

5 Listen and look at 1. Say yes or no.

6 Look at 1. Ask and answer.

Where's the bath?

It's in the bathroom.

THINK BIG What rooms in a house do we use for washing?
What rooms in a house do we use for eating?

7 Listen and read. How many cousins has Jamie got?

5 Jamie, where's the TV?

It's in the living room.

6 Great! They're watching TV. They're quiet!

8 **Look and write.**

> bedroom   living room   kitchen

1 Jamie's cousins are in the _____.

2 Now they're in Jamie's _____.

3 The TV is in the _____.

THINK BIG My father's brother is my...
My father's sister is my...
My uncle's son is my...

9 Listen. Help Jamie and Jenny make sentences.

57

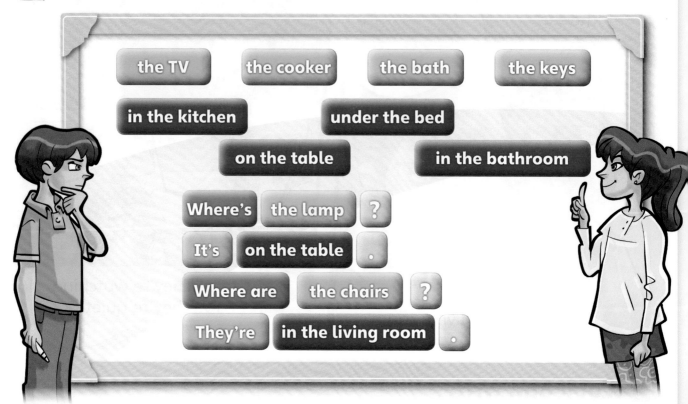

the TV   the cooker   the bath   the keys

in the kitchen   under the bed

on the table   in the bathroom

Where's | the lamp | ?

It's | on the table | .

Where are | the chairs | ?

They're | in the living room | .

10 Look and write. Use **Where's** or **Where are.**

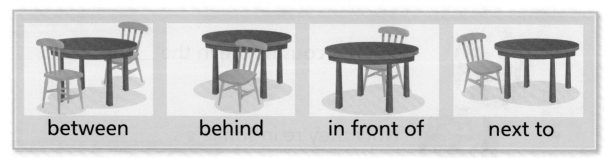

between   behind   in front of   next to

1 _____ the table?
  It's _____ the TV and the sofa.
2 _____ the lamps?
  They're _____ the sofa.
3 _____ the chair?
  _____ the table.
4 _____ the TV?
  _____ the table.

58
11 Listen and stick. Then ask and answer.

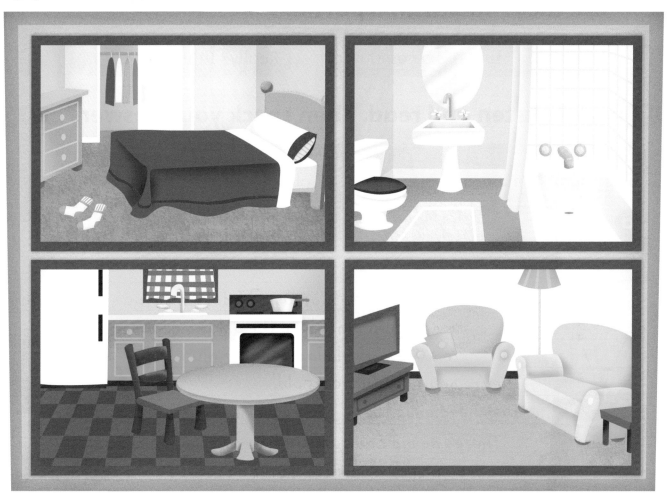

Where are Ben's shoes?

Ben's shoes are in the kitchen.

12 Write and draw. Where's your uncle's phone?

My uncle's phone is

_____

_____ .

Content Connection | History

13 Look at the pictures in 14. What are they? Talk with a partner.

bike   computer   lamp   TV

I think Picture b is a computer.

Really? I think it's a TV.

14 Look, listen and read. Then check your answers in 13.

CONTENT WORDS
burn   museum   new   oil   old   screen   wheel

Emma White

At the Museum

1   Do you like going to museums? I do! My favourite museum is the Science Museum. I love the old things there. There are some very old lamps in the museum. They're nearly 2,000 years old. They need oil in them. The oil burns.

2   There's an old computer in the museum, too. You can put a new computer on a desk or in a backpack but this computer needs a big room.

3   This old TV in the museum is very funny. It's big but the screen is small. I don't want it in my living room!

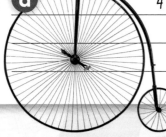

4   My favourite thing in the museum is an old bike. One of its wheels is very big and one wheel is very small. When you ride it, you sit on the big wheel. It's great!

THINK BIG Name one old and one new thing in your classroom and home.

42 Unit 3

15 **Look at 14. Circle T for true and F for false.**

1 Emma likes museums.	**T**	**F**
2 The lamps in the museum are old.	**T**	**F**
3 You can put the old computer in a backpack.	**T**	**F**
4 The old TV has got a big screen.	**T**	**F**
5 Emma wants the old TV in her living room.	**T**	**F**
6 Emma likes the bike in the museum.	**T**	**F**

16 **Old or new? Play a game.**

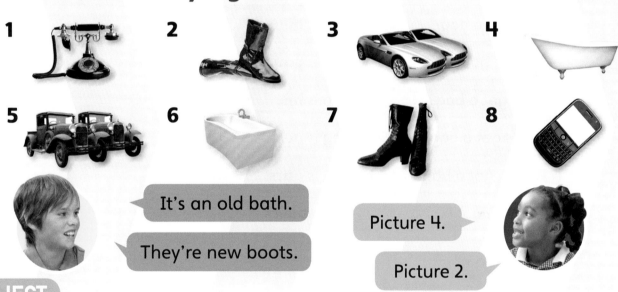

1 2 3 4

5 6 7 8

It's an old bath.

They're new boots.

Picture 4.

Picture 2.

PROJECT

17 **Make an Old and New poster. Then present it to the class.**

Old

New

Ye Olde Manuscript

This car is old. This jacket is new. I like this new car.

61

18 **Listen and read. Then say.**

Mum: Come on, girls! Where are your coats? Jack's wearing his.

Carla: We can't find ours.

Mum: Yours is there, Carla, under the table.

Carla: No, it isn't. That's Anna's coat. Hers is red. Mine is blue.

Mum: Oh, dear! Look! The dogs think your coat is theirs!

19 **Read. Then circle the words in 18.**

I've got a bag.	The bag is **mine**.
You've got a bag.	The bag is **yours**.
He's got a bag.	The bag is **his**.
She's got a bag.	The bag is **hers**.
We've got a bag.	The bag is **ours**.
They've got a bag.	The bag is **theirs**.

I'm wearing my coat. ✔
I'm wearing **my**. ✘

Look at the coats. Mine is red and yours is blue. ✔
Mine coat is red and **yours coat** is blue. ✘

20 **Read and circle.**

1 Eva's got a hat. Is this hat **hers** / **her**?

2 Batu and Jim have got a boat. Is that boat **their** / **theirs**?

3 You've got a green pen. Is this green pen **yours** / **your**?

4 We've got lots of books. Are those books **our** / **ours**?

21 **Read and write.**

I've got a big bedroom at home. I share it with my
sister. Her bed is pink and ¹_____ (I) is green.
My cupboard is brown and ²_____ (she) is black.
Sometimes my cousins play in our bedroom. There are
some games under my bed. Some of the games are
³_____ (we) and some are ⁴_____ (they). My
favourite game is Cluedo. What's ⁵_____ (you)?

Jessie

22 **Read and match.**

1 That's my phone. → That phone is   yours.
2 These are his keys. → These keys are   mine.
3 This is your dog. → This dog is   his.

23 **Look and write. Then compare and say.**

What's your favourite...?	colour	toy	sport
me			
	green	puppet	gymnastics
	red	dinosaur	volleyball
	blue	train	ice skating

Her favourite colour is green.   Mine is pink!

Household Objects

1 In Sudan, some people keep their food cold in clay pots. They put one pot in another, with wet sand between them. A fridge needs electricity but these pots don't. They can keep food cold anywhere.

2 Some people in Mali cook with a solar cooker. A solar cooker doesn't need fuel. It uses the sun. When this cooker is in the sun, it's very hot and it cooks the food quickly. This woman is cooking yam.

24 **Look at the pictures. Then match.**

It's a different bed.	It's a different cooker.
It's a different fridge.	They're different chairs.

25 **Listen and read. Then match and write 1–4.**
62

It can go in a cupboard. ☐   They're Japanese. ☐

It keeps food cold. ☐   It works quickly. ☐

26 **Look at 25. Read and circle.**

1 The clay pots **need / don't need** electricity.

2 The sand between the pots is **dry / wet**.

3 The solar oven needs **fuel / sun**.

4 The Japanese chairs haven't got **arms / legs**.

5 People with hammocks in Sarawak **use / don't use** beds.

3 Do you like these chairs? This is a restaurant in Japan. The chairs haven't got legs, but they're comfortable and Japanese people like them.

4 Some people in Sarawak, Indonesia, sleep in hammocks. They don't use beds. The hammocks are clean and comfortable. When you don't need them, you can put them in a cupboard.

27 **Find the words. Then write.**

At home, we keep food cold in a **1**_____.
When we cook food, we use an **2**_____.
When we eat dinner, we sit on **3**_____s.
We sleep in **4**_____s.

THINK BIG **Do you want the things in the pictures in your home? Why/Why not?**

64

28 **Listen and write. Then say.**

> sink   toy box
> washing machine

1 I put my toys in the _____.

2 I put my dirty dishes in the _____.

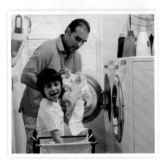

3 I put my dirty clothes in the

_____.

29 **How do you keep your home tidy? Act it out. Then guess.**

> You put your clothes in the cupboard.

THINK BIG Is it good to be tidy at home? Why?
Is it good to be tidy in class? Why?

66
30 **Listen, look and repeat.**

1 OO   **2** OO

67
31 **Listen and find. Then say.**

moon

boo**k**

zoo

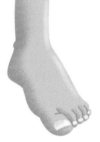

foo**t**

68
32 **Listen and blend the sounds.**

1 r-oo-m   room   **2** l-oo-k   look

3 f-oo-d   food   **4** c-oo-k   cook

5 c-oo-l   cool   **6** g-oo-d   good

69
33 **Underline oo and** oo**. Then listen and chant.**

Look in my cook book.
The food is good!
The food is cool!

34 **Look and choose a room. Draw a line.**

keys

phone

football

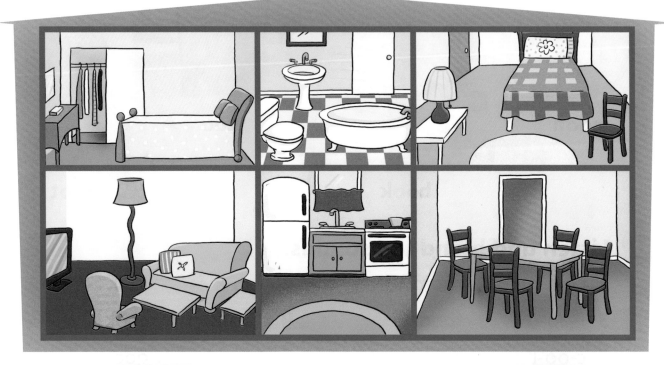

glasses

skates

hat

35 **Look at 34. Ask and answer.**

Where are the keys?

They're on the table in front of the bed.

36 **Look and write. Use old or new.**

baths
chairs
cooker
dressing table
fridge
lamp

1 This _____
is _____.

2 This _____
is _____.

3 This is a _____
_____.

4 This is a _____
_____.

5 These _____
are _____.

6 These are _____
_____.

37 **Read and write.**

brother's   his   mine   yours

James: Leyla, are these glasses on the table _____?

Leyla: No, they're my _____ glasses. I'm wearing _____!

James: Oh, yes! Is this your brother's book?

Leyla: Yes, that's _____.

I Can

☐ **say where things are.**

☐ **talk about possessions.**

☐ **talk about new and old objects.**

Do I Know It?

1 Think about it. Look and circle. Practise.

😊 I know this. 😟 I don't know this.

1			😊 😟	p. 4
2			😊 😟	p. 20
3			😊 😟	p. 36
4			😊 😟	p. 36

5	What's he doing? He's reading a book.	😊 😟	p. 8
6	How many computers are there? There's one computer./There are three computers.	😊 😟	p. 9
7	Don't stand on the table. Be careful!	😊 😟	p. 12
8	What do they like doing? They like flying kites.	😊 😟	p. 24
9	I like volleyball. I don't like tennis.	😊 😟	p. 28
10	She doesn't like swimming. Me neither!	😊 😟	p. 28
11	Where's the table? It's in the kitchen.	😊 😟	p. 40
12	Is this yours? Yes, it's mine.	😊 😟	p. 44

71

2 Get ready.

A Look, listen and write.

between   on   under

Miss Davis:	What's your favourite game in the playground?
Beth:	Mine is football.
Adam:	I like playing ¹_____ the swings.
Katy:	And I like skating!
Miss Davis:	OK. Where's the football?
Beth:	It's ²_____ the chair.
Miss Davis:	And where are Katy's skates?
Adam:	They're ³_____ the two chairs.
Miss Davis:	OK, everybody. Take your things and go outside. And be quick!

B Look at **A** and point. Ask and answer with a partner.

What's she doing?   She's colouring a picture.

C Look at **A**. Point and say how many. Use **There's** or **There are**.

chairs   football   teacher

3 **Get set.**

 Cut out the cards on page 181.
Now you're ready to **Go!**

4 **Go!**

A Look at the cards and write. Listen and check.

> are   colouring   on   reading   they're   under

1 In pictures 1 and 2, they're _____ a picture.

2 In pictures 3 and 4, _____ playing football.

3 In pictures 1 and 3, they're _____ a book.

4 In pictures 2 and 4, there's a basketball _____ the table.

5 In pictures 1, 2, 3 and 4, there _____ keys _____ the table.

B Point to a card. Ask and answer with a partner.

> What do they like doing?

> They like playing football.

> Where are the keys?

> They're on the table.

5 **Write or draw.**

All About Me

What do you like doing in your classroom?	Where do you like reading?
What do you like doing in the playground?	What don't you like?

Do I Know It Now?

6 **Think about it.**

A Go to page 52. Look and circle again.

B Tick (✔).

☐ I can start the next unit.

☐ I can ask my teacher for help and then start the next unit.

☐ I can practise and then start the next unit.

7 **Rate this Checkpoint. Colour the stars.**

 easy   hard   fun   not fun

Units 1–3 Exam Preparation

– Part A –

 Listen and draw lines. There is one example.

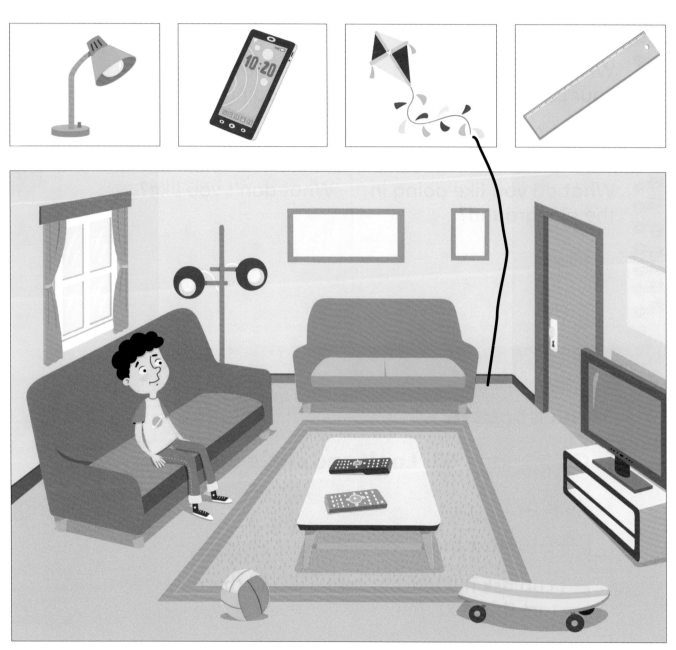

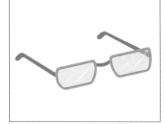

– Part B –

Look and read. Write *yes* or *no*.

Examples

A boy is climbing a tree.	*yes*
There's a blue kite in the tree.	*no*

Questions

1 There's a girl on a bike.   _____

2 Two girls are playing football.   _____

3 A man is listening to music.   _____

4 A woman is running behind a cat.   _____

5 There are two trees.   _____

In My Town

74
1 Listen, look and say.

1 cinema

2 petrol station

3 restaurant

4 train station

5 bus stop

6 post office

7 bookshop

8 computer shop

9 supermarket

10 shopping centre

11 bank

75
2 Listen, find and say. **3** Play a game.

4 Listen and sing. Then look at 1 and find.

Maps Are Great!

Where's the bookshop?
I want to buy a book.
Here, I've got a map.
Come on. Let's take a look!

The bookshop is in River Street.
It isn't far from us.
Do you want to walk there?
No, thanks! Let's take the bus!

I want to send a letter, too.
Is there a post office?
Do you know?
I'm looking at the map.
Yes, there is.
It's near the bookshop.
Come on. Let's go.

Maps are really great.
I use them every day.
In town or out of town,
They help me find my way!

5 Listen and number.

6 Look at 5. Ask and answer.

Where's the restaurant?

It's in Castle Road. It's next to the petrol station.

THINK BIG What can you see at a bus stop?
What can you eat in a restaurant?

7 80 **Listen and read. Where are Jenny and her dad?**

Is There a Bookshop?

1

Do you want to come to the shopping centre, Jenny?

Yes, OK.

2

I want to buy a book. Is there a bookshop?

Yes, there is. Look!

3

I want to buy a computer game. Is there a computer shop?

Yes, there is. It's here.

4

I'm hungry. Let's eat first.

OK. There are restaurants over there!

8 Look and read. Write.

1 Jenny's dad wants to buy a book at the _____.

2 Jenny wants to buy a _____ _____ at the computer shop.

3 Jenny and her dad want to eat lunch at a _____.

4 Jenny wants pizza and _____.

5 Dad hasn't got his _____.

THINK BIG
Do you like shopping?
Where do you go shopping?
What's your favourite shop?
What do you like buying?

9 Listen. Help Jamie and Jenny make sentences.

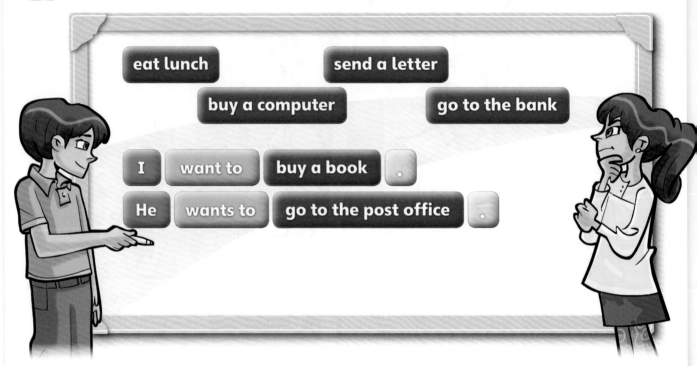

eat lunch		send a letter
	buy a computer	go to the bank

I | want to | buy a book | .

He | wants to | go to the post office | .

10 Write want to or wants to.

1 Mum _____ buy bananas.

2 I _____ buy a new jacket.

3 My brother and I _____ eat sandwiches.

4 Toprak and Richard _____ watch a film.

5 We _____ go to the bus stop.

6 My cousin _____ buy a football.

7 They _____ go to the bank.

8 I _____ send a letter.

11 Listen and stick. Then say.

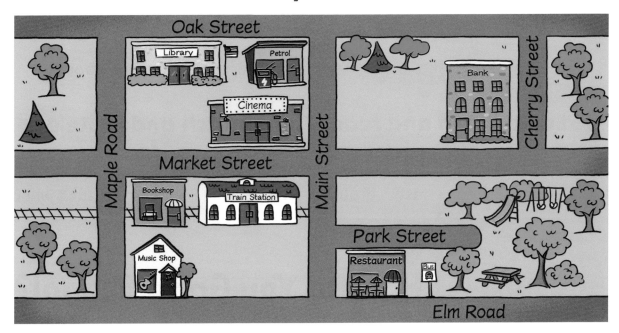

12 Look at 11. Ask and answer.

Is there a bank near here?

Is there a post office in Elm Road?

Yes, there is. It's in Cherry Street.

No, there isn't. It's in Park Street next to the park.

13 Write and draw. Where's the shopping centre?

The shopping centre is

_____

_____

_____ .

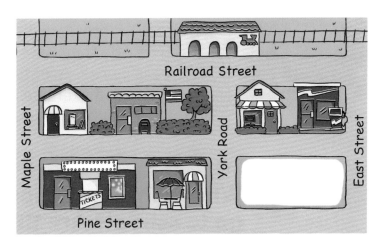

Look at pictures a–d in 15. Which transport do you use? Talk with a partner.

> I use bikes and trains.

> Me, too! I don't use boats.

83
15 **Look, listen and read. Then match and write a–d.**

CONTENT WORDS

boat   canal   fast   ground   safe   slow   underground   without

a

b

c

d

How Do You Go to School?

1 I live in Bangkok and I go to school by boat. There are lots of canals here and there are lots of boats on the canals.

Sunan

2 Here in Mexico City, there are lots of cars on the roads. Going by car is slow. I always go to school by bus. It's fast and the bus stop is near my school.

Carmen

3 I go to school by underground train. It goes under the ground. There are lots of underground trains here in New York and there are 468 stations! One of the stations is very near our flat.

Sophia

4 I live in Amsterdam and I go to school by bike. My friends ride their bikes, too. There are lots of "bike streets" here – streets without cars. They're safe and it's good exercise.

Lars

THINK
BIG **What other transport can you use to go to school? Are they fast or slow?**

16 **Look at 15. Read and write the names.**

1 _____ exercises on his way to school.

2 _____ lives near a station.

3 _____ goes to a school with a bus stop near it.

4 _____ lives in a place with lots of canals.

5 _____ lives in a place with safe streets for bikes.

6 _____ goes under the ground on her way to school.

17 **Do a class survey. Ask and answer.**

	bus	train	boat	bike	other
Sam	✔				

Sam, how do you go to school?

I go to school by bus.

PROJECT

18 **Make a Go to School bar chart. Then present it to the class.**

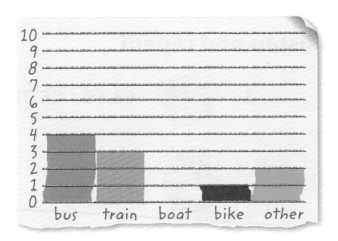

In my class, four children go to school by bus.

Listen and read. Then say.

Shop assistant:	Hello. Can I help you?
Mary:	Yes, please. How much is this pencil case?
Shop assistant:	It's six euros.
Mary:	And how much are those notebooks?
Shop assistant:	They're three euros and fifty cents.
Mary:	Can I buy a green notebook, please?

20 **Read. Then circle How much, euros and cents in 19.**

How much	is	it? this pencil case? that train?
	are	they? these pens? those notebooks?

It's	twelve **euros**. twenty-five **cents**.
They're	four **euros** and fifty **cents**.

A hundred cents (100c) = one euro (€1).

 Listen and circle. Then listen and repeat.

1 29c / 99c

2 €3.50 / €5.30

3 €3.90 / €9.90

4 €13 / €23

22 **Look and write.**

1    €8
2    €19.50
3    €3
4   €9.99

1 How much is the ball?
   It's _____ euros.
2 How much are the shoes?
   They're _____ euros and _____ cents.
3 _____ _____ is the hat?
   It's _____ _____.
4 _____ _____ is the game?
   _____ _____ _____ and
   _____-_____ _____.

23 **Read and number in order.**

☐ **A:** OK.
☐ **B:** Yes, please. How much are these biscuits?
☐ **A:** They're two euros and thirty-five cents.
☐ **A:** Hi. Can I help you?
☐ **B:** Can I buy them, please?

24 **Look at 22 and 23. Role play.**

Hello. Can I help you?

Yes, please. How much are...?

Taxi!

There are taxis in every city in the world but they aren't all the same. Here are some of our favourites.

1 **In London**, most of the taxis are big and black. They have a famous design. They're modern but they look like cars from a long time ago. They're comfortable and fun to ride in.

2 **In Berlin**, taxis are comfortable but they aren't very colourful. They're very light brown, with a black and yellow taxi sign on top. Most of them look the same.

25 **Look at the pictures. What kind of car do they show?**

26 **Listen and read. Then match and write a–d.**

88

27 **Read again. Then circle T for true and F for false.**

1 Havana has got some old taxis. T F

2 The big black taxis in London aren't very old. T F

3 The taxis in Berlin are all different colours. T F

4 All the taxis in New Delhi have got three wheels. T F

THINK BIG Why do people take taxis? Which taxi in the pictures do you like? Why?

3 **In New Delhi**, lots of taxis have only got three wheels! They're green and yellow and they've got a special name: tuk tuk. They aren't very fast but they're cheap and easy to find. ☐

4 **In Havana**, there are lots of colourful taxis. Some of them are old but these black and yellow taxis are new and modern. They've got three wheels and they're really fun. ☐

28 **Complete for a city you know. Then write.**

Name of city _____

Taxis   old ☐   new ☐   big ☐   small ☐

colour(s) _____

Buses   old ☐   new ☐   big ☐   small ☐

colour(s) _____

In New York, there are lots of taxis. They're big and new. Most of them are yellow. There are lots of buses, too. Most of them are blue and white but school buses are yellow.

In..., there are lots of...
They're...
Most of them are...

90
(29) Listen and write. Then say.

cross look wait

1 First, I always _____ at the pedestrian crossing.

2 Second, I _____ for the green man.

3 Last, I _____ left, then right, then left again before I cross the road.

30 Look and number. Then ask and answer.

a

b

c

How do you cross the road safely?

First, I always cross at the pedestrian crossing.

THINK BIG What is a zebra crossing? Find out. Why is it called a zebra crossing?

Listen, look and repeat.

1 ai   **2** oa

 Listen and find. Then say.

train

rain

boat   **coat**

 Listen and blend the sounds.

1 n-ai-l   nail   **2** oa-k   oak

3 t-ai-l   tail   **4** s-oa-p   soap

5 w-ai-t   wait   **6** r-oa-d   road

 Underline ai and oa. Then listen and chant.

Wear a coat
To sail the boat!
Drive the train
In the rain!

35 **Work in two groups. Make sentence cards.**

Group A:
Write sentences starting with *I want to*. Write a different activity for each pupil in the group.

Group B:
Write sentences starting with *There's a*. Write a different place for each pupil in the group.

36 **Groups A and B: Take turns to read your cards. Find your match.**

I want to buy a book.

Yes, a match!

There's a bookshop near here.

37 **Read and match.**

1 I want to buy a book.
2 Erol wants to see a film.
3 Mum and Dad want to put petrol in the car.
4 Ben wants to send a letter.

a There's a cinema near the bus stop.
b There's a post office in Main Street.
c There's a bookshop in Maple Road.
d There's a petrol station next to the bank.

38 **Look and write. Use by.**

1 Many children go to school
_____.

2 My sister comes home
_____.

3 My mum goes to the bank
_____.

39 **Read and circle.**

Maria: Mum, **I want / wants** to buy a ruler.
Mum: **How many / How much** is it?
Maria: It's two **euro ten cents / euros and ten cents**.
Mum: OK.

I Can

☐ say what I want and talk about money.
☐ describe where places are in town.
☐ talk about different kinds of transport.

unit 5

My Dream Job

97

1 Listen, look and say.

1 actor

2 artist

3 dancer

4 doctor

5 writer

6 pilot

7 singer

8 athlete

9 teacher

10 chef

11 vet

98

 2 Listen, find and say.   **3** Play a game.

4 Listen and chant. Then look at 1 and find.

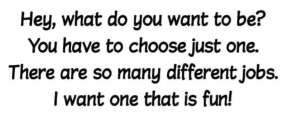

Hey, What Do You Want to Be?

Hey, what do you want to be?
You have to choose just one.
There are so many different jobs.
I want one that is fun!

I want to be a dancer
And an athlete, too.
Or maybe a teacher.
What about you?

I want to be an actor
And I want to be a vet.
I want to be a pilot, too.
Then I can fly a jet!

Chorus

5 Listen and write.

1 I want to be a _____.

2 I want to be a _____.

3 I want to be a _____.

6 Look at 1. Ask and answer.

What do you want to be?

I want to be a chef.

THINK BIG What jobs do people do at school?
What jobs do people do in town?

7 103

Listen and read. What does Jamie like doing?

Dream Jobs!

What do you want to be, Jenny?

I want to be a singer. I like singing.

1

What do you want to be, Dan?

I want to be a writer. I like writing stories.

2

What's your dream job, Maria?

I want to be a dancer. I like dancing.

3

Jamie, your sister wants to be a singer. What do you want to be?

I want to be a chef.

4

8 **Look at the story. Write.**

1 Jenny wants to be a _____.
2 Dan wants to be a _____.
3 Maria wants to be a _____.
4 Jamie wants to be a _____.

THINK BIG **What's your favourite job in the story? Why?**
What do you want to be? Why?

Language in Action

9 Listen. Help Jamie and Jenny make sentences.

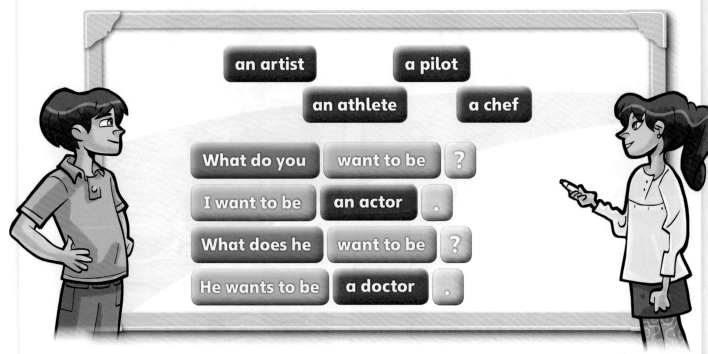

| an artist | a pilot |
| an athlete | a chef |

What do you | want to be | ?

I want to be | an actor | .

What does he | want to be | ?

He wants to be | a doctor | .

10 Look and write. Then draw and write.

1 What does she want to be?

_____

2 What does he want to be?

_____

3 What does Sally want to be?

_____

4 What do you want to be?

_____

105
11 **Listen and stick. Then say.**

1

2

3

4

12 **Look at 11. Ask and answer.**

What does he want to be?

He wants to be a singer.

13 **Write. Use do or does.**
1 What _____ he want to be?
2 What _____ they want to be?
3 What _____ your cousins want to be?
4 What _____ your brother/sister want to be?

14 Look at the pictures in 15. What are the jobs? How do they help us?

106
15 Look, listen and read. Then circle.

> **CONTENT WORDS**
> carpenter   entertain   farmer   hairdresser
> look after   nurse   produce   provide   waiter

Goods and Services

Businesses want to make money. There are two ways to do this. They can produce goods or they can provide services.

1   **Goods** are products. They're things that people buy and sell. Food, clothes, cars, books and houses are goods. There are virtual goods, too, for example electronic books that you can read on a tablet. When a farmer grows food or a carpenter makes a table, they're producing goods.

2   **Services** are activities that people do for others. When a hairdresser cuts your hair or a nurse looks after you, they're providing a service. Actors and singers provide a service, too: they entertain you.

3   Some businesses provide goods and services together. For example, a restaurant sells goods: the food and drink. But it provides services, too: the waiters take the food to the table and other people wash the dishes after the meal.

growing food:
goods / services
cutting hair:
goods / services
a restaurant:
goods / goods and services

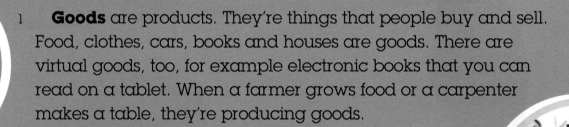

THINK BIG Do people in these jobs produce goods, provide services or both?
pilot   artist   baker

16 **Look at 15. Circle T for true and F for false.**

1 Businesses make money with goods and services.   **T**   **F**

2 People buy and sell goods.   **T**   **F**

3 Services are products.   **T**   **F**

4 Actors produce goods.   **T**   **F**

5 Waiters wash the dishes in a restaurant.   **T**   **F**

17 **Look and match. Then ask and answer.**

actors	take	ill people
waiters	grow	food to tables
hairdressers	look after	food
farmers	cut	people
nurses	entertain	hair

What do actors do?

They entertain people.

18 **Make a Goods and Services poster. Then present it to the class.**

Here are some goods: milk, a table...

Goods

Services

milk   a table

flying a plane

19 **Listen and read. Then say.**

Harry:	Hi, Jasmine. Do you want to go to the park?
Jasmine:	Sorry, I can't. I'm with my dad at the mechanic's because our car isn't working.
Harry:	Oh, well. Maybe I can go with Gemma or Adnan.
Jasmine:	No, Adnan is at the hairdresser's because he wants a new hairstyle. And Gemma is at the vet's because her dog looks ill.
Harry:	Oh, dear! Maybe we can go tomorrow…

20 **Read. Then circle because in 19.**

Tim wants to be a doctor. He loves Science.
→ Tim wants to be a doctor **because** he loves Science.

Gemma is at the vet's. Her cat looks ill.
→ Gemma is at the vet's **because** her cat looks ill.

The weather **looks nice**. Let's have a picnic.
You **look tired**. Are you OK?

21 **Read and match.**

1 She's at the doctor's   **a** because she's a chef.
2 She's at school   **b** because her computer isn't
3 She's at the bank   working.
4 She's at a restaurant   **c** because she needs money.
5 She's at the computer   **d** because she's a teacher.
   shop   **e** because she feels ill.

22 **Read and circle.**

1 My uncle goes to a restaurant every day because he's **a doctor** / **a waiter**.

2 My sister wants to be a nurse because she loves to **help people** / **grow food**.

3 David wants to be **a carpenter** / **a hairdresser** because he loves to make things.

4 I think that man is **an actor** / **a carpenter** because he looks funny.

5 I think that woman is a nurse because **she looks kind** / **she looks ill**.

23 **Look and write. Use because.**

| at the beach | at the hairdresser's |
| at the supermarket | in the kitchen |

1 She's _____ she wants a new hairstyle.

2 They're _____ they need food.

3 He's _____ he wants to be a chef.

4 She's _____ she loves the sea.

24 **Draw and write.**

I'm _____

_____

(where?) because

_____

_____

(why?).

When I Grow Up

What do you want to be when you're older? These kids know.

1   I'm José Antonio. My home is near the ocean in Costa Rica. I love swimming and looking at the colourful fish here. My mum is a photographer. I sometimes use her underwater camera. It takes great photos. When I grow up, I want to be a scuba diver and work underwater.

25 Look at the photos. Find the jobs.

park ranger   rodeo rider   scuba diver

26 Listen and read. What do they like?

27 Look at 26. Read and circle.

1 José Antonio likes **swimming / catching fish**.

2 Katie's family has got lots of **children / cows**.

3 **Juma / Juma's** father is a park ranger.

THINK BIG Which jobs help animals in your city? What do you want to be? Why?

2   My name's Katie. I'm from Oklahoma, in the United States. My family lives on a ranch and we've got lots of cows and horses. I love our ranch. When I finish school, I want to be a vet and help animals. In my free time, I want to ride in the rodeo!

3   My name's Juma. I live with my family in Botswana, in Africa. I love the beautiful animals here. Some of them are in danger. This is a picture of my father. One day, I want to be a park ranger like him and help protect wild animals.

28 **Ask three friends. Then write.**

What do you want to be?

What do farmers do?

I want to be a farmer.

They grow food and work with animals.

Name	What/want to be?	What/do?

29 **Listen and write. Then say.**

| Art | Maths | Music | Science |

1 I like _____.
I want to be a teacher.

2 I like _____.
I want to be a doctor.

3 I like _____.
I want to be a pilot.

4 I like _____.
I want to be an artist.

30 **Tell a partner what you want to be. Then act it out.**

I like Music. I want to be a singer.

I like Music, too. I want to be a dancer.

THINK BIG You like _____. What other jobs can you do?
a Art **b** Music **c** Maths **d** Science

112 **31 Listen, look and repeat.**

1 ar   **2** er   **3** or

 113 **32 Listen and find. Then say.**

arm   **car**

teacher   **corn**

 114 **33 Listen and blend the sounds.**

1	c-ar-t	cart	**2**	s-i-ng-er	singer
3	f-or	for	**4**	ar-t	art
5	b-or-n	born	**6**	l-e-tt-er	letter

 115 **34 Underline ar, er and or. Then listen and chant.**

I want to be a singer
Or an artist painting art.
I want to be a teacher
Or a farmer with a cart!

35 Work in small groups. Ask "What do you want to be?". Write names and jobs.

Name	Wants to Be
Michael	a pilot

36 Count how many pupils in 35 want each job. Write a list.

Job	How Many
Doctor	3

37 Look at this bar chart. Make a bar chart for your group and talk about it.

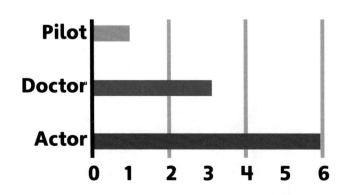

One pupil wants to be a pilot. Three pupils want to be doctors.

38 **Look and write.** | dancer singer teacher writer |

1 _____ 2 _____ 3 _____ 4 _____

39 **Read and match.**

1 I want to protect animals.
2 I want to look after people.
3 I want to grow food.
4 I want to work in the water.

a I want to be a nurse.
b I want to be a lifeguard.
c I want to be a farmer.
d I want to be a park ranger.

40 **Write.**

1 What does she want to be?

_____

because _____.

2 What does he want to be?

_____

because _____.

3 What do you want to be?

_____

because _____.

I Can

☐ **talk about jobs.**
☐ **say what I want to be and why.**
☐ **talk about studying hard and setting goals.**

My Day

unit 6

1 **Listen, look and say.**

1:00 one o'clock **2:00** two o'clock **3:00** three o'clock **4:00** four o'clock

5:00 five o'clock **6:00** six o'clock **7:00** seven o'clock **8:00** eight o'clock

9:00 nine o'clock **10:00** ten o'clock **11:00** eleven o'clock **12:00** twelve o'clock

2 **Listen, find and say.** **3** **Play a game.**

4 Listen and sing. Then look at 1 and find.

What Time Is It?

Tick, tock. It's seven o'clock.
Time to get up and get dressed.
I want to stay in bed
But it's time to brush my teeth!

Tick, tock. It's eight o'clock.
At nine o'clock I start school.
I eat my breakfast and get my books.
I love school, it's cool!

Tick, tock. It's three o'clock.
There's no more school today.
I do my homework and I go out.
And there's my friend to play.

Now it's evening and it's eight o'clock
And it's time to go to bed.
I watch TV and read my book.
Time to sleep now, good night!

5 Look at 4. Listen and say yes or no.

6 Look at 1. Ask and answer.

What time is it?

It's one o'clock.

THINK BIG
What time is it now?
What time is it at midday?
What time is it at midnight?

7 **Listen and read. When does Max get up?**

Max's Day

1 Mum, I get up at seven o'clock. When does the cat get up?

2 Max gets up at two o'clock in the afternoon. Then he eats and goes out.

3 When does Max come back?

He comes back at seven o'clock, then he sleeps again.

4 I do my homework at four o'clock. Then I play and watch TV.

8 ## Look at the story. Number in order.

- [ ] Max comes home.
- [ ] Max gets up.
- [ ] Max eats.
- [ ] Max sleeps again.
- [ ] Max goes out.

THINK BIG **What time do you go to bed?**
What time do you get up?
How many hours do you sleep? Is that good or bad?

125

9 Listen. Help Jamie and Jenny make sentences.

| go out | start school | watch TV | finish school |

| at 9:00 | at 7:00 | at 3:00 | at 12:00 |

| When | does he get up | ? |

| He gets up | at 6:00 | . |

| When | do you go to bed | ? |

| I go to bed | at 8:00 | . |

10 Look and write do or does. Then answer the questions.

1 When _____ she eat lunch?

She _____

_____.

2 When _____ they go to school?

They _____

_____.

3 When _____ he brush his teeth?

He _____

_____.

11 **Listen and stick. Then say.**

1

2

3

4

12 **Look at 11. Ask and answer.**

 When does she go to bed?

She goes to bed at nine o'clock.

13 **Look and write. Use start and finish.**

1 When does the film start?
It starts at
_____.

2 When does the film finish?
It finishes at
_____.

3 When _____ school _____?
_____
_____

4 _____
_____?
_____
_____

14 Look at the pictures in 15. What do all the things do?
128

15 Look, listen and read. Then match and write a–d.

CONTENT WORDS
burn   candle   cup   fall   height   hourglass   sand   shadow   sundial

a

Telling the Time

b

What time is it? How do you know? Today we look at clocks, watches and mobile phones but here are some other ways to tell the time. Some are very old.

1 A sundial uses the sun to tell the time. The sun makes a shadow on the sundial and the shadow tells the time. It's a great invention but it isn't useful at night or when it's cloudy! ☐

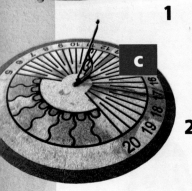

c

d

2 A candle clock can work in the day or at night. When the candle burns, it gets shorter. The height of the candle tells you the time. ☐

3 An hourglass uses sand to tell the time. Sand falls from the top to the bottom. Some people use small hourglasses today when they're cooking eggs. ☐

4 A water clock uses water to tell the time. It works like an hourglass. It's got two cups. The water falls from one cup to the other. ☐

THINK BIG Look, think and draw.

16 Look at 15. Read and circle.

1 A sundial uses **a shadow / clouds** to tell the time.

2 A sundial **works / doesn't work** at night.

3 The candle in a candle clock changes **height / colour**.

4 People **use / don't use** hourglasses now.

5 A water clock uses water and **sand / cups** to tell the time.

17 What is it? Choose and play a game.

candle   cup   hourglass   sand   sundial   water clock

It uses the sun to tell the time.

A sundial!

You drink with it.

A cup!

PROJECT

18 Make a Clock poster. Then present it to the class.

This is a cuckoo clock. It uses a cuckoo to tell the time. It's eleven o'clock in this picture.

Cuckoo! Cuckoo!

19 **Listen and read. Then say.**

Journalist:	Who are you?
Steve Radcliff:	I'm Steve Radcliff.
Journalist:	What's your job?
Steve Radcliff:	I'm a teacher.
Journalist:	Where do you work?
Steve Radcliff:	In a school in London.
Journalist:	How do you get to work?
Steve Radcliff:	By train and bus.
Journalist:	When do you work?
Steve Radcliff:	I work from Monday to Friday and sometimes on Saturday.
Journalist:	How many pupils are there in your class?
Steve Radcliff:	Thirty-five. It's enough for me!

 Read. Then circle the question words in 19.

question word	possible answers	topic
who	*Steve Radcliff, my mum*	people
what	*job, table*	things
when	*on Saturday, every day*	time
where	*at home, in a school*	place
how	*by train, by bus*	manner
how many	*three, thirty-five*	number

do questions: Where do you work? How does he get to work?
am/is/are questions: Who are you? Where's your coat?

21 Read and match.

1 Who is she?
2 What does she do?
3 Where does she sell the stories?
4 How do you get to town?
5 When is the bookshop open?

a At the bookshop.
b She writes stories.
c By bus.
d Jane Bowling.
e Every day.

22 Read and circle.

1 **A: What / Where** is that?   **B:** It's Marisa's T-shirt.

2 **A: When / How many** is your party? **B:** Today!

3 **A: How / How many** dolls have you **B:** Only one.
   got?

4 **A: How / What** do you play tennis? **B:** You hit a ball.

5 **A: When / Where** are you going?   **B:** My grandma's house.

23 Write. Use question words and do, is or are.

1 **A:** _____ ____ your friends?   **B:** Leyla, Erol and Fatih.

2 **A:** _____ ____ you live?   **B:** In Turkey.

3 **A:** _____ ____ your favourite   **B:** Pasta.
   food?

4 **A:** _____ ____ you go to school? **B:** By bike.

5 **A:** _____ ____ you have English   **B:** On Wednesday.
   lessons?

24 Look at 23. Ask and answer for you.

Who are your friends?   Sophie and Bill.

My Day

All around the world, children eat, play and go to school but some children have got very different routines from others.

Bruno, Brazil

1   I get up at 6 o'clock and I go to school from 7 o'clock to 12 o'clock. Then I go home for a big lunch with my family. In the afternoon, I play with my friends or go to a dance class. I love dancing! Dinner is at 8 o'clock. After that, I'm very tired and I go to bed.

25 **How many hours are you at school every day? Is it a long time?**

26 **Listen and read. Whose day is like yours?**

131

27 **Look at 26. Then circle T for true and F for false.**

1 Bruno goes to school in the afternoon.   **T F**

2 Jun eats with her mum and dad in the evening. **T F**

3 Ali goes to bed in the afternoon.   **T F**

THINK BIG **Is a long school day good or bad? Why?**

Jun, China

2   My school starts at 8 o'clock and finishes at 5 o'clock but we have a break for two hours at lunch time. I have dinner with my mum and dad at 7 o'clock. When I finish my homework, I like watching TV.

Ali, Egypt

3   I go to school from Sunday to Thursday because Friday is a holiday here. Classes start at 8 o'clock. At 10 o'clock we have a break and school finishes at 3 o'clock. I play with my sisters in the afternoon and we go to bed at 9 o'clock.

28 **Look and complete. Then write.**

My Perfect School Day

activity	time
get up	
	before school
start school	
	at break
finish school	
	after school
have dinner	
go to bed	

I get up at seven o'clock. I eat breakfast before school.

133

29 **Listen and number in order. Then say.**

a

I get dressed quickly
and eat breakfast.

b

I always get to school
on time.

c

I get my backpack ready
the night before school.

d

I get up early on
school days.

30 **Tell your partner how you get to school on time.
Do the actions.**

I get up early
on school days.

 **We all come to school at the same
time. Why is this good?
What other things is it good to be
on time for? Why?**

31 **Listen, look and repeat.**

1 ch   **2** tch   **3** sh

 32 **Listen and find. Then say.**

fish   **witch**   **chin**   **ship**   **rich**

 33 **Listen and blend the sounds.**

1 ch-o-p   chop   **2** sh-o-p   shop

3 m-a-tch match   **4** l-u-n-ch lunch

5 d-i-sh   dish   **6** w-a-tch watch

 34 **Underline ch, tch and sh. Then listen and chant.**

Watch the witch,
She's having lunch!
Fish and chips
At the shop!

35 **Play the Silly Sentences game.**

First, write times on cards. Then write daily activities on other cards.

Now work in groups. Make two piles of cards. Take turns. Turn over one card from each pile and read a silly sentence.

36 **Look and write. What time is it?**

1 It's _____. **2** It's _____. **3** It's _____.

4 It's _____. **5** It's _____. **6** It's _____.

37 **Read and match.**

1 Where is   **a** you eat for dinner?

2 Who are   **b** do you wake up?

3 What do   **c** Jane's book?

4 When   **d** your mum's best friends?

38 **Find and write the words.**

1 An _____ uses sand to tell the time. (galhossru)

2 A _____ uses the sun to tell the time. (ladsuin)

3 A water _____ uses water to tell the time. (ccolk)

4 We use clocks and _____ to tell the time. (swtaech)

I Can

☐ talk about times and daily activities.

☐ ask questions.

☐ talk about different ways of telling time.

Do I Know It?

1 **Think about it. Look and circle. Practise.**

😊 I know this. 😕 I don't know this.

1				😊 😕 p. 58
2				😊 😕 p. 74
3				😊 😕 p. 90
4				😊 😕 p. 94

5 He wants to buy a book.	😊 😕	p. 62
6 Is there a cinema near here? Yes, there is./No, there isn't.	😊 😕	p. 63
7 How much is that pen? It's two euros and fifty cents.	😊 😕	p. 66
8 What do you want to be? I want to be a pilot.	😊 😕	p. 78
9 I want to be a doctor because I love Science.	😊 😕	p. 82
10 I think she's a nurse because she looks kind.	😊 😕	p. 82
11 When does she get up? She gets up at seven o'clock.	😊 😕	p. 94
12 Who's that? Where are you? What's your job?	😊 😕	p. 98

139

2 Get ready.

A Look, listen and write.

> artist   athlete   do   does   teacher   where

Charlie: Hey, Linda, what do you want to be?

Linda: I want to be an ¹_____ because I love sport.

Charlie: Really? What ²_____ your sister want to be?

Linda: She wants to be an ³_____.

Charlie: Why?

Linda: Well, my uncle is an artist. It's his job.

Charlie: ⁴_____ does he work?

Linda: He works at home. He draws pictures for books. What ⁵_____ you want to be, Charlie?

Charlie: I want to be a ⁶_____ because I like school!

B Talk about what you want to be. Say why.

What do you want to be?

I want to be a vet.
I like animals.

1
2
3
4
5
6
7
8
9

3 Get set.

STEP 1 Cut out the cards on page 183.

STEP 2 Put the cards on your desk. Mix the cards up.
Now you're ready to **Go!**

4 Go!

A Take turns with a partner. Pick up a card. Continue until
you find a matching card. Read your cards aloud.

I want to buy a book.

Is there a bookshop
near here?

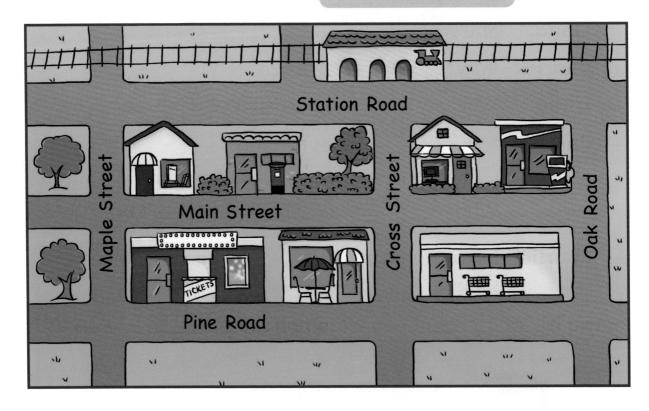

B Hold up one card at a time and find it on the map.
Ask and answer.

Where's the bookshop?

It's in Main Street.

5 **Write or draw.**

All About Me

What do you want to be? Why?	What time do you start school?
Where's your school?	When do you go to bed?

Do I Know It Now?

6 **Think about it.**

A Go to page 106. Look and circle again.

B Tick (✔).

☐ I can start the next unit.

☐ I can ask my teacher for help and then start the next unit.

☐ I can practise and then start the next unit.

7 **Rate this Checkpoint. Colour the stars.**

 easy   hard   fun   not fun

1
2
3
4
5
6
7
8
9

Units 4–6 Exam Preparation

– Part A –

 Listen and tick (✔) the box. There is one example.

Where is the bookshop?

 A ☐    B ✔    C ☐

1 What does Kim want to buy?

 A ☐    B ☐    C ☐

2 How does Nick go to school?

 A ☐    B ☐    C ☐

3 What time is it now?

 A ☐    B ☐    C ☐

4 Who's Anna's dad?

 A ☐    B ☐    C ☐

5 What time does the boy get up?

 A ☐    B ☐    C ☐

– Part B –

Read this. Choose a word from the box. Write the correct word next to numbers 1–5. There is one example.

Lucy wakes up at _____eight_____ o'clock every day. She gets dressed and eats 1_____ in the kitchen. Then she brushes her 2_____. Lucy plays the 3_____ all day. Then she 4_____ out. She doesn't like cooking. She eats dinner in a 5_____ next to her house.

What's Lucy's job?
She's a singer.

example			
eight	restaurant	chef	teeth
goes	breakfast	guitar	bus stop

My Favourite Food

1 Listen, look and say.

1 bananas

2 apples

3 strawberries

4 tomatoes

5 carrots

6 potatoes

7 oranges

8 mangoes

9 cheese

10 yoghurt

11 vegetables

12 sandwiches

13 burgers

14 snack

15 meat

142

2 Listen, find and say.   **3** Play a game.

4 **Listen and sing. Then look at 1 and find.**

Let's Eat Lunch!

It's twelve o'clock.
Let's eat lunch.
Do you like bananas?
I like them for lunch!

Do you like tomatoes?
Yes, I do. I like tomatoes. I really do.
Do you like potatoes?
Yes, I do. I like potatoes, too. Do you?

Meat and fruit,
Vegetables and snacks,
I like them all.
Can I have more, please?

Have some chips
And a burger, too.
Let's share some ice cream.
I like eating lunch with you!

5 **Listen, match and write.**

I like _____.

I like _____.

I like _____.

1

2

3

a

b

c

 6 **Look at 1. Ask and answer.**

Do you like bananas?

Yes, I do. I like bananas.

THINK BIG **Which pictures show fruit?**
Which pictures show vegetables?

Story

7 Listen and read. Does Dan like apples?

8 Look at the story. Write yes or no.

1 Does Dan like fruit? _____

2 Does Jamie like bananas? _____

3 Does Dan like mangoes? _____

4 Do the boys like pie? _____

5 Is it a banana pie? _____

THINK BIG **What fruit do you like?**
What dishes can you make with fruit?

9 Listen. Help Jamie and Jenny make sentences.

sandwiches	carrots and potatoes

yoghurt   cheese

Do you | like | fruit | ?

Yes, I do. I | like | apples and bananas | .

Does she | like | vegetables | ?

No, she doesn't. She doesn't | like | vegetables | .

10 Look and write. Then answer.

1 _____ she like strawberries?

Yes, she _____. She _____ strawberries.

2 _____ he like tomatoes?

No, he _____. He _____ tomatoes.

3 _____ they like sandwiches?

Yes, they _____. They _____ sandwiches.

4 Do _____ like oranges?

_____, I _____. I _____ oranges.

11 **Listen and stick. Then say.**

1

2

3

4

12 **Look at 11. Ask and answer.**

Do you like strawberries?

No, I don't. I like apples.

13 **Draw and write. Do you like vegetables?**

_____

_____

_____

14 **Look at the pictures. Which snacks can you name?**

15 **Look, listen and read. Then circle.**

> **CONTENT WORDS**
>
> diabetes   disease   fat   healthy   heart
> label   salt   sugar   too much   unhealthy

Healthy and Unhealthy Snacks

Healthy food helps us grow and keeps us from getting ill. Some snacks are healthy but others are not very healthy. Unhealthy snacks have got too much sugar, fat or salt in them.

1 Sugar

Sugar gives us energy but when we don't use all that energy, it makes us fatter. Sugar is bad for our teeth and can give us diabetes. Sweets have got a lot of sugar in them.

2 Fat

Like sugar, fat gives us energy. When we eat too much of it, it stays in our body and makes us fatter. It can give us heart disease. Chocolate has got a lot of fat in it.

3 Salt

Salt doesn't make us fatter but too much of it can give us heart disease. Crisps have got a lot of salt in them.

Many snacks have got labels that say how much sugar, fat and salt is in them. Your mum or dad can help you read the label and choose healthy snacks.

sweets:
a lot of **sugar** / **salt**

chocolate:
a lot of **fat** / **salt**

crisps:
a lot of **sugar** / **salt**

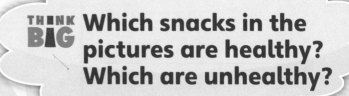

THINK BIG **Which snacks in the pictures are healthy? Which are unhealthy?**

16 **Look at 15. Read and match.**

1 Healthy food   a give us energy.
2 Sugar and fat   b is bad for our teeth.
3 Fat and salt   c tell us how much fat, sugar and
4 Too much sugar   salt is in snacks.
5 Labels   d helps us grow.
                  e can give us heart disease.

17 **Look. Then ask and answer.**

	chips	cakes	strawberries
sugar	★	★ ★ ★	★
fat	★ ★ ★	★ ★ ★	★
salt	★ ★ ★	★	★

Have chips got a lot of sugar in them?   No, they haven't.

PROJECT

18 **Make a Healthy and Unhealthy Snacks poster. Then present it to the class.**

Unhealthy   Healthy

a lot of fat and salt

a lot of fat and sugar

not much fat, sugar or salt

This salad is a healthy snack. It hasn't got much fat, sugar or salt in it.

19 Listen and read. Then say.

Mum:	Do you want some pasta for dinner, Ella?
Ella:	Yes, please. And before that, can I have some fruit?
Mum:	Sure. You can have an apple or a pear...
Ella:	No, thanks. I want some strawberries and some blueberries.
Mum:	OK. That's a very healthy snack!
Ella:	No, I'm not eating them, Mum. I'm making a picture with them.
Mum:	Oh, Ella! That looks amazing!

20 Read. Then circle **a, an and some** in 19.

Countable	Uncountable
• Apple, snack and book are countable.	• Pasta and water are uncountable.
• We can count these things (1 apple, 2 apple**s**, 3 apple**s**...).	• We can't count these things (pasta, water...).
	• These words don't change.
• We use **a/an/some** with these words.	• We use **some** with these words.

21 Circle the things you can count.

1 meat **2** milk **3** carrot **4** salt

5 biscuit **6** sugar **7** sandwich **8** potato

22 **Read and circle.**

1 **Joe:** Can I have **a / some** juice, please?

Mum: Sorry, no, but you can have **a / some** water.

2 **Mum:** Do you want **a / some** burger for dinner?

Joe: Yes, please. Can I have **an / some** orange for dessert?

23 **Read and write a, an, or some.**

Kemal: I want ¹_____ meat, please. Can I have
²_____ big potato, too?

Waiter: Of course. And what about dessert? Would you
like ³_____ orange?

Kemal: No, thanks. I want ⁴_____ banana.

24 **Look. Choose three things. Then ask and answer.**

Do you want some cheese?　　No, thanks.

Do you want a biscuit?　　Yes, please.

watermelon

Where Fruit Comes From

Fruit is a very healthy snack. But where does it come from?

1   Watermelons come from South Africa. Turkey and China also grow a lot of watermelons and they're very popular in Japan. In Japan, they haven't only got round watermelons. They've got square ones, too!

pineapple

25 **Look at the fruit. Which do you like to eat?**

154
26 **Listen and read. Then match.**

1 Pineapples   **a** South Africa

2 Watermelons   **b** China

3 Avocados   **c** South America

4 Kiwis   **d** Mexico

Supermarkets sell fruit from around the world. How do you know where it comes from?

kiwi

2   Pineapples grow in tropical countries, such as in South America. There are lots of pineapple plants in the Philippines and people there make fabric for clothes from pineapple leaves.

3   Kiwis are China's national fruit! They come from China but now they grow in many parts of the world, like Italy and New Zealand. Their skin is ugly but inside they're beautiful.

4   Many avocados come from Mexico but they're popular all over the world. In Indonesia, people make a sweet drink with avocado, milk, sugar and sometimes chocolate.

avocado

27 **Look at 26. Read and write.**

| avocados   kiwis   pineapples   watermelons |

1 You can eat _____ and the leaves are useful, too.

2 _____ can be round or square.

3 _____ are a national fruit.

4 New Zealand grows a lot of _____.

5 People make a sweet drink with _____.

6 _____ are popular in Japan.

155
28 **Listen and say true or false. Then play a game.**

Pineapples come from South Africa.

False! They come from Brazil.

culture connection (fruit) Unit 7 **123**

157

29 **Listen and number. Then write and say.**

a **b** **c** **d**

apple
biscuit
carrots
crisps

I want an _____, please.

No _____ for me, thanks.

Just one _____, please.

I like _____.

30 **Look and circle. Then look at 29 and role play.**

1

healthy / unhealthy

2

healthy / unhealthy

3

healthy / unhealthy

4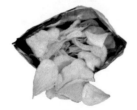

healthy / unhealthy

5

healthy / unhealthy

6

healthy / unhealthy

I want a carrot, please.

No chocolate for me, thanks.

THINK BIG **What healthy food did you eat today?**
What unhealthy food did you eat today?

31 **Listen, look and repeat.**

1 ee   **2** ie

 32 **Listen and find. Then say.**

sheep   **bee**

pie   **tie**

 33 **Listen and blend the sounds.**

1 f-ee-t   feet   **2** l-ie   lie

3 s-ee   see   **4** f-l-ie-s   flies

5 ch-ee-se cheese   **6** c-r-ie-d   cried

34 **Underline ee and ie. Then listen and chant.**

"See the cheese!"
Cried the bees.
"See the pies!"
Cried the flies.

35 **Play the What Do You Like? game.**

1 Circle yes for the foods you like. Circle no for the foods you don't like.
2 Guess what your partner likes. Circle.
3 Your partner says what he or she likes. Tick (✓) your correct guesses.

	YOU		YOUR PARTNER		CORRECT?
1 carrots	yes	no	yes	no	
2 cheese	yes	no	yes	no	
3 tomatoes	yes	no	yes	no	
4 mangoes	yes	no	yes	no	
5 oranges	yes	no	yes	no	
6 burgers	yes	no	yes	no	
7 sandwiches	yes	no	yes	no	
8 meat	yes	no	yes	no	
9 strawberries	yes	no	yes	no	
10 potatoes	yes	no	yes	no	

Greg, do you like carrots?

Greg likes carrots. He doesn't like cheese.

Yes, I do.

36 **Tell the class what your partner likes and doesn't like.**

37 **Look and write. Use a, an and some.**

1 She's eating _____ biscuit.

2 They're eating _____ sandwiches.

3 He's drinking _____ milk.

4 He's eating _____ ice cream.

38 **Find and write the words.**

1 _____ come from Africa. (meWtalnosre)

2 _____ come from Mexico. (sadvoAco)

3 _____ come from China. (wiiKs)

4 _____ come from South America. (sipplPneae)

I Can

☐ talk about food.

☐ talk about healthy and unhealthy food.

☐ say where fruit comes from.

Wild Animals

 1 Listen, look and say.

1 giraffe

2 hippo

3 kangaroo

4 cheetah

5 polar bear

6 zebra

7 parrot

8 monkey

9 peacock

10 elephant

11 crocodile

12 snake

164
 2 Listen, find and say.   **3** Play a game.

4 Listen and sing. Then look at 1 and find.

To the Zoo!

I really like animals!
Do you like them, too?
That's why I'm so happy.
We're going to the zoo!

A kangaroo can jump.
A monkey can jump, too.
Crocodiles can chase
And swim.
And you, what can you do?

A giraffe can't fly or jump up high.
An elephant can't climb trees.
Fish can't run and hippos can't fly.
Come and see them.
Oh, yes, please!

Now it's time to say goodbye
To every animal here.
But we can come back
And see them every year!

5 Listen and say true or false.

6 Look at 1. Ask and answer.

Do you like cheetahs?

Yes, I do!
Cheetahs can run.

THINK BIG Which animals can chase other animals?
Which animals can climb trees?

7 Listen and read. What animals does Jamie like?

8 **Look. Circle can or can't.**

1 Monkeys **can** / **can't** climb trees.

2 Monkeys **can** / **can't** jump.

3 Hippos **can** / **can't** climb trees.

4 Hippos **can** / **can't** jump.

5 Hippos **can** / **can't** eat a lot.

6 Jamie **can** / **can't** eat a lot.

THINK BIG **What animals can swim, run and eat fish?**
What animals can't fly or climb trees?

9 170 **Listen. Help Jamie and Jenny make sentences.**

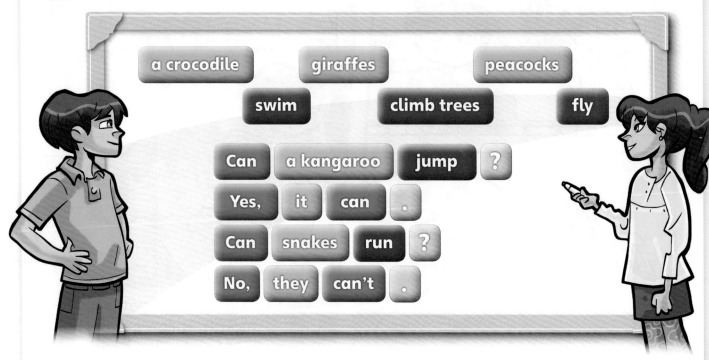

10 Look and write. Then draw and write.

1 _____ a zebra see at night?

Yes, _____.

2 _____ cheetahs run?

Yes, _____.

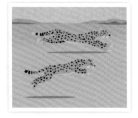

3 _____ a giraffe climb trees?

No, _____.

4 _____

_____

11 **Listen and stick. Then write.**

elephants   kangaroos   monkeys   snakes

1 Can _____ climb trees?

2 Can _____ run?

3 Can _____ play?

4 Can _____ fly?

12 **Look at 11. Ask and answer.**

Can monkeys climb trees?

Yes, they can.

13 **Write and draw. Then say.**

_____

_____

_____

14 Look at the pictures in 15. Which animals can you name?

172

15 Look, listen and read. Then circle.

CONTENT WORDS

cover   desert   forest   fox   jungle
lizard   ocean   raccoon   seal   whale

Animal Habitats

A habitat is the place where an animal lives.

1   The **forest** is a cool, dark habitat with lots of trees. Deer, raccoons and foxes live there. Forests cover ¹ **8%** / **28%** of the planet.

2   ² **6%** / **60%** of our planet is **desert**. It's hot in the day and cold at night. There isn't much rain so it's very dry and there aren't many plants. Lizards and snakes live there.

3   The **ocean** covers ³ **21%** / **71%** of our planet and the water in it is salty. Many kinds of fish live in the ocean. Other animals live there, too, like whales and seals.

4   It's hot in the **jungle** and it rains a lot. Monkeys and colourful birds and butterflies live there. There are tigers, too! The jungle covers only ⁴ **2%** / **12%** of the planet but 50% of all plant and animal species live there.

THINK BIG Which animal habitats are there in your country? Which animals live there?

16 Read again. Then match.

1
Foxes

2
Monkeys

3
Snakes

4
Whales

a live in the ocean.
c live in the forest.

b live in the desert.
d live in the jungle.

17 Think of an animal. Ask and answer.

Can it swim?   Yes.

Does it live in the ocean?   Yes.

Is it a whale?   Yes.

PROJECT

18 Make an Animal Habitats poster. Then present it to the class.

Tigers live in the jungle. It's hot and wet there.

19 Listen and read. Then say.

Jane: Dad's got a nice new camera.
His pictures from the zoo are great!

Sam: Can I see them?

Jane: Of course! Look at this giraffe
with its long black tongue.

Sam: It's really cool! And I love that beautiful young
polar bear.

Jane: Me too, but my favourite animal is this funny green
frog with big red eyes. It's amazing!

20 Read. Then circle the describing words in 19.

Putting describing words in order
1 opinion   2 size/shape   3 age   4 colour
a nice new camera ✓ (a new nice camera ✗)
a long black tongue
a beautiful young polar bear
a funny green frog
big red eyes

21 Look at 20. Read and ✔ or ✗.

1 a long black scarf   ☐

2 a black long scarf   ☐

3 big red boots   ☐

4 a green funny bird   ☐

5 new nice shoes   ☐

22 **Look and write.**

| beautiful | blue | cool | funny | grey | long |
| nice | old | short | small | white | young |

opinion	size/shape	age	colour
amazing	big	new	yellow

23 **Read, order and write.**

1 The _____ _____ (brown, tall) giraffe is eating the _____ _____ (nice, green) leaves.

2 The _____ _____ (blue, old) peacock's got a _____ _____ (green, beautiful) tail.

3 The _____ _____ (brown, big) kangaroo is carrying a _____ _____ (beautiful, young) baby.

24 **Choose the correct clues and draw a monster.**

My monster's got

two big green heads. ☐

two red small heads. ☐

four long funny hands. ☐

four nice small hands. ☐

three new short shoes. ☐

three long old shoes. ☐

On this website, children around the world can share stories and pictures about the amazing animals that live near their homes. Let's take a look.

1   This is a koala. Koalas come from Australia and so do I! This one lives in the gum tree outside my bedroom window. She sleeps a lot but when she isn't sleeping, she's very interesting. She's very slow and she eats and eats.

Vincent, Australia

25 **Look at the pictures. Then match.**

> It can make snowballs.   It sleeps a lot.   It's a pet.

175
26 **Listen and read. Then check your answers in 25.**

THINK BIG Can you see these animals in your country? Where? Which animals are good pets? Why?

2   Every day when I wake up, I see a friendly face in the field outside my window. His name is Papi and he's a llama. He's not a wild llama, he's a family pet. He can jump very high.

Angela, Peru

3   I can see some wonderful animals near my home. They're snow monkeys and they live in the forest. They like making snowballs. I can see them from our car window but I don't go too close. They aren't pets.

Kyoko, Japan

27 Look at 26. Read and match.

Animal	Country	Where does it live?	What does it do?
llama	Peru	a tree	makes snowballs
koala	Japan	the forest	sleeps a lot
snow monkey	Australia	a field	jumps high

28 Complete the chart about an animal that lives near you. Then ask and answer.

What animal is it?	
Where does it live?	
What does it do?	

What animal is it?   A fox.

29 Listen and number. Then say.

a

b

c

d

I think peacocks are beautiful.

Monkeys are so clever.

Giraffes are amazing. Their necks are so long.

Elephants are very strong.

30 Look at 29. Ask and answer.

amazing   beautiful   clever   strong

What animal do you like?

I like parrots. They're so beautiful.

THINK BIG **What's your favourite animal? Why?**

31 **Listen, look and repeat.**

1 OU   **2** OW

 32 **Listen and find. Then say.**

cow

soup

owl

You

you

 33 **Listen and blend the sounds.**

1 g-r-ou-p   group   **2** t-ow-n   town

3 t-ou-c-a-n   toucan   **4** c-l-ow-n   clown

5 d-ow-n   down   **6** r-ou-te   route

 34 **Underline ou and ow. Then listen and chant.**

An owl went
Down to town
To see a group
Of toucans
Drinking soup.

35 Play the What Animal Am I? game.

Step 1. Write the name of an animal on a sticky note. Don't show your partner.

Step 2. Stick your note on your partner's forehead. Your partner asks you questions and guesses the animal.

Step 3. Now play with other partners.

36 **Look and ✔.**

1 a short black skirt ☐
   a black short skirt ☐

2 a blue cool jacket ☐
   a cool blue jacket ☐

3 long nice trousers ☐
   nice long trousers ☐

4 new red boots ☐
   red new boots ☐

5 small funny gloves ☐
   funny small gloves ☐

6 old green shorts ☐
   green old shorts ☐

37 **Read and circle.**

1 Whales live in **jungles** / **oceans**.

2 Monkeys live in **jungles** / **deserts**.

3 Fish live in **forests** / **oceans**.

4 Foxes live in **jungles** / **forests**.

I Can

☐ describe animals.

☐ talk about where animals live.

☐ talk about appreciating animals.

unit 9 Fun All Year

1 Listen, look and say.

January
MON	TUE	WED	THU	FRI	SAT	SUN
1	2	3	4	5	6	7
8	9	10	11	12	13	14
15	16	17	18	19	20	21
22	23	24	25	26	27	28
29	30	31				

February
MON	TUE	WED	THU	FRI	SAT	SUN
			1	2	3	4
5	6	7	8	9	10	11
12	13	14	15	16	17	18
19	20	21	22	23	24	25
26	27	28	29			

March
MON	TUE	WED	THU	FRI	SAT	SUN
			1	2	3	
4	5	6	7	8	9	10
11	12	13	14	15	16	17
18	19	20	21	22	23	24
25	26	27	28	29	30	31

April
MON	TUE	WED	THU	FRI	SAT	SUN
1	2	3	4	5	6	7
8	9	10	11	12	13	14
15	16	17	18	19	20	21
22	23	24	25	26	27	28
29	30					

May
MON	TUE	WED	THU	FRI	SAT	SUN
	1	2	3	4	5	
6	7	8	9	10	11	12
13	14	15	16	17	18	19
20	21	22	23	24	25	26
27	28	29	30	31		

June
MON	TUE	WED	THU	FRI	SAT	SUN
				1	2	
3	4	5	6	7	8	9
10	11	12	13	14	15	16
17	18	19	20	21	22	23
24	25	26	27	28	29	30

July
MON	TUE	WED	THU	FRI	SAT	SUN
1	2	3	4	5	6	7
8	9	10	11	12	13	14
15	16	17	18	19	20	21
22	23	24	25	26	27	28
29	30	31				

August
MON	TUE	WED	THU	FRI	SAT	SUN
	1	2	3	4		
5	6	7	8	9	10	11
12	13	14	15	16	17	18
19	20	21	22	23	24	25
26	27	28	29	30	31	

September
MON	TUE	WED	THU	FRI	SAT	SUN
						1
2	3	4	5	6	7	8
9	10	11	12	13	14	15
16	17	18	19	20	21	22
23	24	25	26	27	28	29
30						

October
MON	TUE	WED	THU	FRI	SAT	SUN
1	2	3	4	5	6	
7	8	9	10	11	12	13
14	15	16	17	18	19	20
21	22	23	24	25	26	27
28	29	30	31			

November
MON	TUE	WED	THU	FRI	SAT	SUN
			1	2	3	
4	5	6	7	8	9	10
11	12	13	14	15	16	17
18	19	20	21	22	23	24
25	26	27	28	29	30	

December
MON	TUE	WED	THU	FRI	SAT	SUN
						1
2	3	4	5	6	7	8
9	10	11	12	13	14	15
16	17	18	19	20	21	22
23	24	25	26	27	28	29
30	31					

2 Listen, find and say. **3** Play a game.

4 Listen and chant. Then look at 1 and find.

I Like July!

July is my favourite month.
I like August, too.
I'm happy and on holiday,
There is so much to do!

I also like September.
That's when I start school.
I'm so excited, aren't you?
My friends will be there, too!

I don't like December.
It is so very cold.
But then it is my birthday, too.
This year, I'm eight years old!

5 Listen and write the month.

1 _____ 2 _____ 3 _____

6 Look at 1. Ask and answer.

What's your favourite month?

I like May.

THINK BIG Which months are holiday months at school?

7 **Listen and read. When is Jamie's birthday?**

Fun in August!

What's your favourite month, Jenny?

JAN. FEB. MAR.
APR. MAY JUNE
JULY AUG. SEPT.
OCT. NOV. DEC.

1 I like December. We always go on holiday in December.

Do you go on holiday in winter?

DECEMBER

2 No, I never go on holiday in winter. It's too cold!

I always go on holiday in August. I love swimming in the sea.

AUGUST

3

What do you do in August, Jamie?

AUGUST

4 I always have fun in August. It's my birthday!

5 I never go to school. I always have a big party!

6 And Mum always makes a big chocolate cake! August is my favourite month!

8 **Look at the story. Circle.**

1 Jenny's favourite month is **January** / **December**.
2 Dan goes swimming in **January** / **August**.
3 Jamie's favourite month is **August** / **May**.
4 Jenny always goes on holiday in **December** / **November**.
5 Dan never goes on holiday in **August** / **December**.
6 Jamie always has a party in **April** / **August**.

THINK BIG **When do you go on holiday?**
I always go on holiday in _____.
I never go on holiday in _____.

Language in Action

9 Listen. Help Jamie and Jenny make sentences.

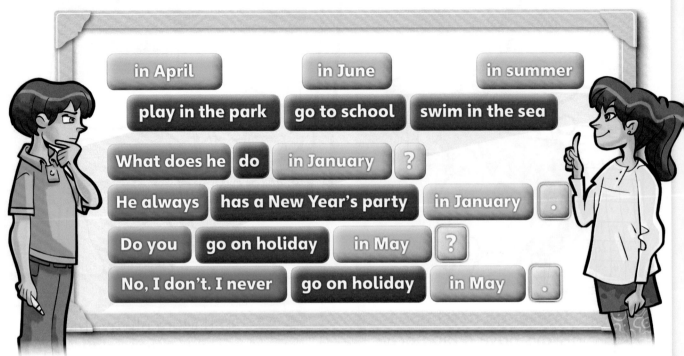

in April   in June   in summer

play in the park   go to school   swim in the sea

What does he do in January ?

He always has a New Year's party in January .

Do you go on holiday in May ?

No, I don't. I never go on holiday in May .

10 Write and circle.

1 What does she do in summer? Does she play tennis?
Yes, she _____. She **always** / **never** plays tennis in summer.

2 What _____ you do in February? Do you go on holiday?
No, we _____. We **always** / **never** go on holiday in February.

3 Do they go to school in September?
Yes, they _____. They **always** / **never** go to school in September.

4 Do you go to the park in winter?
_____. I **always** / **never** go to the park in winter.

11 **Listen and stick. Then write the number.**

a

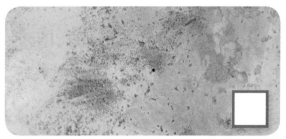

We always swim in the sea.

b

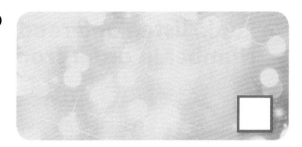

We always go to my grandad's house.

c

We always go on holiday.

d

I always play football with my friends.

12 **Look at 11. Ask and answer.**

Do you go on holiday in April?

No, I don't. I never go on holiday in April.

13 **Write and draw. What do you do in winter?**

I _____

_____

in winter.

Look at the pictures in 15. What are the people doing?

 Look, listen and read. When are the festivals?
Number in order from January.

CONTENT WORDS
celebration   confetti   hang   pole   wish

Celebrating
Special Days

Every country has special days and exciting celebrations. Let's take a look at some of them.

a

People in England celebrate spring on 1st May. On **May Day**, people put flowers and ribbons on a special pole. Children hold the ribbons and dance around the pole.

b

Italy is famous for its **carnivals**. In February and March, there are parties in the streets. People wear masks and children throw small pieces of paper called confetti.

In China, people celebrate the **Mid-Autumn Festival**. This festival happens in September or October when the moon is very big and bright. Children wear colourful masks and dance in the streets. They also eat sweet cakes called mooncakes.

c

In Japan, people celebrate the star festival, **Tanabata**. In July and August, people write wishes on paper. They hang the wishes on bamboo to make a "wish tree".

d

☐ May Day

☐ Mid-Autumn Festival

☐ Carnivals in Italy

☐ Tanabata

THINK BIG **What celebrations are there in your country? What do people do?**

16 Look at 15 and ✔.

	May Day	Carnivals	Mid-Autumn	Tanabata
wear masks				
eat special food				
dance				
make wishes				
throw paper				

17 Look and say. Then ask your friends.

Name	Favourite festival	When?

What's your favourite festival?

National Children's Day.

When do you celebrate National Children's Day?

On 23rd April.

PROJECT

18 Make a Festivals poster. Then present it to the class.

Winter

We celebrate Christmas in winter.

We celebrate Christmas in winter. We have parties and decorate our homes.

Listen and read. Then say.

Tom: Hi, Tom. How are you?

Joe: Great, thanks! I love winter holidays.

Tom: What's the weather like there?

Joe: It's snowing. It's very cold but I like it. What's the weather like at home?

Tom: It's raining. I hate days like this!

Joe: What are you doing?

Tom: I'm writing a story. In my story, it's always summer. It's always hot and sunny in summer!

20 **Read. Then circle the words in 19.**

It's **hot**.		It's **raining**.	
It's **cold**.		It's **snowing**.	
It's **sunny**.			

 Listen and circle. Then listen and repeat.

1 London:  **2** Paris:

3 New York: **4** Mexico City:

22 **Put the words in order. Then say.**

1 like | the weather | What's | there?

2 cold | It's | and rainy. | very

3 in the summer. | It's | hot | always

4 like it. | It's | but I | very cold,

5 sunny | today. | It's hot | and

6 What's | weather | the | in | like | New York?

23 **Look. Then ask and answer.**

Jan–Feb	Mar–Apr	May–Jun	Jul–Aug	Sep–Oct	Nov–Dec

24 **Imagine. Then draw and write.**

1 What month is it?
   It's _____.

2 What's the weather like?
   It's _____.

3 What are you doing?
   I'm _____.

New Year's Eve

People all over the world celebrate New Year's Eve on the night of 31st December. It's the last day of the year and there are lots of parties. But the celebrations at midnight are very different in different places.

1 In Spain, people eat twelve grapes at twelve o'clock – one with every chime of the clock. People think that the grapes bring good luck for the next year. Then there are fireworks.

 25 **Is New Year special in your country? What do you do?**

197
 26 **Listen and read. Then match.**

1 Spain   **a** listen to something

2 Scotland   **b** sing a song

3 Japan   **c** eat fruit

THINK BIG **What do people in your country do when they want good luck? Do you think it works?**

2 In Scotland, New Year's Eve is called Hogmanay. At midnight, people hold hands and sing a special song about old friends. Then they visit their friends' and family's homes. The first person through the door gives a piece of coal to bring good luck to the family.

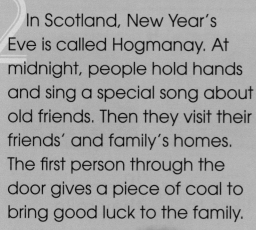

3 In Japan, people eat a special noodle soup on New Year's Eve for good luck. They eat the soup and listen to a bell ring 108 times at midnight. They believe the bell takes away 108 bad things before the New Year.

27 **Look at 26. Circle T for true and F for false.**

1 People in Spain eat grapes on New Year's Eve.　　T　F
2 In Scotland, singing a song brings good luck.　　T　F
3 In Japan, people eat 108 noodles for good luck.　T　F

28 **Look, answer and write.**

New Year's Eve in My Country
On New Year's Eve in ¹_____,
we wear ²_____. We eat
³_____. We celebrate
⁴_____ with ⁵_____.
At midnight, we ⁶_____.

1 Which country?
2 Ordinary clothes?
　Special clothes?
　What kind and colour?
3 What foods?
4 Where?
5 Who?
6 What do you do?

199

29 **Listen and write the season. Then say.**

autumn spring winter summer

1 **2** **3** **4**

In _____, they skate on ice.

In _____, he rides his bike.

In _____, she likes to swim.

In _____, they rake leaves.

30 **Draw and write. What do you do in each season?**

1 In summer, _____

_____ .

2 In winter, _____

_____ .

31 **Look at 30. Ask and answer.**

What do you do in winter?

In winter, I do gymnastics.

THINK BIG What can you only do in winter? Why?
What can you only do in summer? Why?

200

32 Listen, look and say.

Aa   Bb   Cc   Dd   Ee
Ff   Gg   Hh   Ii   Jj
Kk   Ll   Mm   Nn   Oo
Pp   Qq   Rr   Ss   Tt
Uu   Vv   Ww   Xx   Yy   Zz

 201

33 Listen, look and chant. Can you find something starting with every letter of the alphabet?

A, B, C, D, E, F, G.
I can see an ant and a bat. What can you see?
H, I, J, K, L, M, N, O, P.
I can see a hat and some ink. What can you see?
Q, R, S, T, U, V.
I can see a rat and a snake. What can you see?
W, X, Y and Z.
I can see six yellow wolves and a zebra, I said!

34 **Play the Months Line-Up game.**

Step 1. Ask when your classmates' birthdays are. Then line up in order by month.

> When's your birthday?

> It's in November. When's yours?

> My birthday's in July.

Step 2. Check the order with the class.

> My birthday's in August.

> My birthday's in November.

> My birthday's in January.

Step 3. Play the game again. Ask and answer. Then line up again by month.

1 What's your favourite month?
2 What's your favourite holiday?
3 When's your favourite school event?

35 **Look and match for your country.**

October

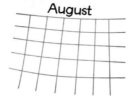
August

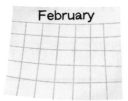
February

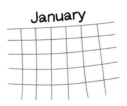
January

a

b

c

d

36 **Write about you.**

1 What do you do in winter?
I always _____ in winter.
I never _____ in winter.

2 What do you do in summer?
I always _____ in summer.
I never _____ in summer.

3 What do you do in autumn?
I always _____ in autumn.
I never _____ in autumn.

4 What do you do in spring?
I always _____ in spring.
I never _____ in spring.

I Can

☐ **talk about what I do each month.**

☐ **talk about the weather.**

☐ **talk about seasonal holidays.**

Do I Know It?

1 **Think about it. Look and circle. Practise.**

😊 I know this.   ☹ I don't know this.

#		
1		p. 112
2		p. 128
3		p. 144
4		p. 145
5	Does she like fruit? Yes, she does./No, she doesn't.	p. 116
6	I want a pizza, some chips and some salad.	p. 120
7	Can snakes jump? Yes, they can./No, they can't.	p. 132
8	I've got a nice new jacket and big brown shoes.	p. 136
9	What does he do in January? He always has a New Year's party in January.	p. 148
10	Do you go on holiday in winter? Yes, we do./ No, we don't. We never go on holiday in winter.	p. 149
11	What's the weather like? It's raining and cold.	p. 152

I Can Do It!

204
2 **Get ready.**

A Look, listen and write.

> always   an   can   can't   never   pet   some

Alan: That's a beautiful green parrot. Is it yours?

Tess: Yes. His name is Crackers. He's my
¹_____ . He's very clever. He
²_____ talk!

Alan: He can?

Tess: Yes, he can.

Alan: That's amazing! Look: I've got ³
_____ apple and ⁴_____
nuts. Does he like fruit?

Tess: Yes, he does. He loves it!

Alan: Ha, ha.

Tess: He can sing, too.

Alan: Really?

Tess: Yes. He ⁵_____ sings
to me in the morning!

Alan: Wow. My cat's so boring. She
⁶_____ say anything and
she ⁷_____ sings to me!

B Look at A. Ask and answer.

> What can Crackers do?

> What can't
> Alan's cat do?

> Does Crackers
> like fruit?

1
2
3
4
5
6
7
8
9

3 Get set.

STEP 1 Cut out the outline on page 185. Cut each card in half along the dotted line.

STEP 2 Sort the cards into two piles. Put the heads of the animals in one pile and the bodies in the other. Now you're ready to **Go!**

4 Go!

A Put one card from each of your piles together to make a funny animal.

B Talk about your funny animals. Ask and answer.

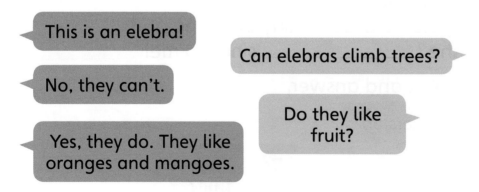

This is an elebra!

Can elebras climb trees?

No, they can't.

Do they like fruit?

Yes, they do. They like oranges and mangoes.

C Look at others' animals. Who's got the same animal as you?

5 **Write or draw.**

All About Me

When's your birthday?	What's the weather like today?
What's your favourite month?	What do you always do in summer?

1

2

3

4

5

6

Do I Know It Now?

6 **Think about it.**

A Go to page 160. Look and circle again.

B Tick (✔).

☐ I can ask my teacher for help.

☐ I can practise.

7 **Rate this Checkpoint. Colour the stars.**

easy   hard

fun   not fun

7

8

9

– Part A –

205

Read the question. Listen and write a name or a number. There are two examples.

Examples

What's the girl's name?	*Grace*
How old is she?	6

Questions

1 What's Grace's friend's name? _____

2 Which class are they in? _____

3 How many parrots has Grace got? _____

4 What's the name of Grace's favourite parrot? _____

5 How many children are there in Grace's class? _____

– Part B –

Look at the pictures and read the questions.
Write one-word answers.

Examples

How many hippos are there?   _____ one _____

Where's the crocodile?   under a ___ tree ___

Questions

1 What's the crocodile doing?   it's _____

2 Where's the monkey now?   on the girl's _____

3 What's the monkey taking?   an _____

4 How many children are looking at the parrot? _____

5 What can the parrot do?   it can _____

Young Learners English Practice Starters: Listening A

– 5 questions –

 Listen and tick (✓) the box. There is one example.

What's Alex doing?

A ☐

B ✔

C ☐

1 What's Jill doing?

A ☐

B ☐

C ☐

2 What's Ben doing?

A ☐

B ☐

C ☐

3 Where's Pat's jacket?

A ☐

B ☐

C ☐

4 How many people are in the picture?

A ☐

B ☐

C ☐

5 What are Bill and Ann doing?

A ☐

B ☐

C ☐

Young Learners English Practice Starters: Listening B

– 5 questions –

Read the question. Listen and write a name or a number. There are two examples.

Examples

What is the boy's name?   _Tom_

How old is he?   _10_

Questions

1 How old is Sara? _____

2 How many books has Tom got? _____

3 What's the cat's name? _____

4 What's the dog's name? _____

5 Where's the library? in _____ Street

Young Learners English Practice Starters: Listening C

– 5 questions –

 Listen and draw lines. There is one example.

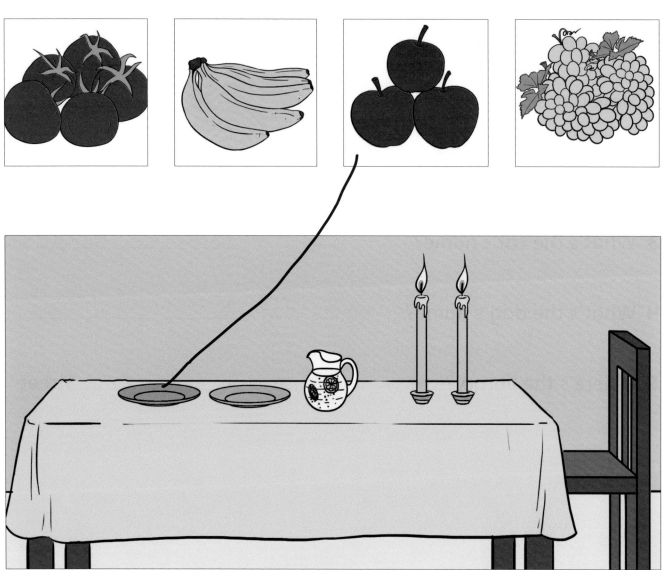

Young Learners English Practice Starters: Reading & Writing A

– 5 questions –

Look at the pictures. Look at the letters. Write the words.

Example

<u>s w i n g</u>　　　　g w i n s

Questions

1

_ _ _ _ _ _ _ _　　　r e t m o c u p

2

_ _ _ _ _　　　d e s l i

3

_ _ _ _ _ _ _ _ _ _　　　t a s k e d r a b o

4

_ _ _ _ _ _　　　n e c l i p

5

_ _ _ _ _ _ _　　　r e t i c u p

Young Learners English Practice Starters: Reading & Writing B

– 5 questions –

**Look and read. Put a tick (✓) or a cross (✗) in the box.
There are two examples.**

Examples

She is a doctor. ✔

This is a bus stop. ✗

Questions

1

This is a bookshop. ☐

2

She is a dancer. ☐

3

He is a teacher. ☐

4

This is a petrol station. ☐

5

He is a singer. ☐

Young Learners English Practice Starters: Reading & Writing C

– 5 questions –

Read this. Choose a word from the box. Write the correct word next to numbers 1–5. There is one example.

A Zoo

I am a big place. A lot of animals live in me. The _elephant_ has got big ears and a long trunk. The ¹_____ is a bird with a beautiful tail. The ²_____ is another beautiful bird. It likes talking. Then there are ³ _____. They've got long tails and live in my trees. The ⁴_____ is a large grey animal with small ears. It likes the water. And the ⁵_____ has got a long neck and spots. What am I? I am a zoo.

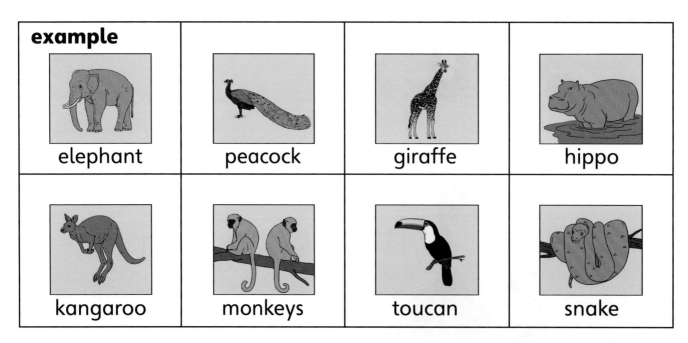

example			
elephant	peacock	giraffe	hippo
kangaroo	monkeys	toucan	snake

Wordlist

Unit 1	Page
classroom	4
colouring	4
counting	4
cutting	4
gluing	4
listening	4
playing a game	4
using the computer	4
watching a DVD	4
writing	4
equals	10
minus	10
one hundred	10
plus	10
in a forest	14
in a garden	14
in the mountains	14
on a boat	14
take turns	16
bath	17
both	17
crocodile	17
Maths	17
mouth	17
path	17
teeth	17
then	17
thin	17
with	17

Unit 2	Page
climbing trees	20
doing gymnastics	20
flying kites	20

ice skating	20
playing tennis	20
playing volleyball	20
riding my bike	20
skateboarding	20
like	21
love	21
playground	21
running	21
swing	21
together	22
team	23
bones	26
exercise	26
feet	26
fingers	26
jump	26
kick	26
move	26
muscles	26
strong	26
take care of	26
throw	26
weak	26
each side	32
helmet	32
in front of	32
knee pads	32
safely	32
slide	32
seesaw	32
bang	33
bank	33
ink	33
king	33

ring	33
sink	33
wing	33

Unit 3	Page
bath	36
bathroom	36
bed	36
bedroom	36
chair	36
cooker	36
cupboard	36
dressing table	36
DVD player	36
fridge	36
kitchen	36
lamp	36
living room	36
sink	36
sofa	36
table	36
TV	36
behind	37
glasses	37
in	37
keys	37
on	37
put on	37
aunt	38
cousin	38
uncle	38
quiet	39
between	40
in front of	40
next to	40

under	40	computer shop	58	pedestrian crossing	70
phone	41	petrol station	58	right	70
bike	42	post office	58	second	70
burn	42	restaurant	58	wait	70
computer	42	shopping centre	58	drive	71
museum	42	supermarket	58	nail	71
new	42	town	58	oak	71
oil	42	train station	58	rain	71
old	42	buy	59	sail	71
screen	42	eat	59	soap	71
wheel	42	far	59	tail	71
clay	46	letter	59	wear	71
dry	46	map	59		
electricity	46	near	59	**Unit 5**	**Page**
fuel	46	send	59	actor	74
household	46	first	60	artist	74
solar	46	hungry	60	athlete	74
wet	46	wallet	61	chef	74
comfortable	47	film	62	dancer	74
hammock	47	boat	64	doctor	74
dirty	48	canal	64	dream job	74
dishes	48	fast	64	pilot	74
tidy	48	go to school by	64	singer	74
toy box	48	ground	64	teacher	74
washing machine	48	safe	64	vet	74
cook	49	slow	64	writer	74
cool	49	underground	64	carpenter	80
moon	49	design	68	entertain	80
zoo	49	famous	68	farmer	80
		long time ago	68	grow	80
Unit 4	**Page**	sign	68	hairdresser	80
bank	58	taxi	68	nurse	80
bookshop	58	cross the road	70	produce	80
bus stop	58	last	70	provide	80
cinema	58	left	70	take care of	80

Wordlist

waiter	80	burn	96	mangoes	112
ill	81	candle	96	meat	112
park ranger	84	cup	96	oranges	112
rodeo rider	84	fall	96	potatoes	112
scuba diver	84	height	96	sandwiches	112
help	85	hourglass	96	snack	112
protect	85	sand	96	strawberries	112
Art	86	shadow	96	tomatoes	112
Maths	86	sun	96	vegetables	112
Music	86	sundial	96	yoghurt	112
Science	86	tell the time	96	chips	113
set goals	86	use	96	fruit	113
study hard	86	water clock	96	ice cream	113
arm	87	work	96	share	113
born	87	routine	100	pie	115
cart	87	tired	100	chocolate	118
corn	87	after school	101	diabetes	118
letter	87	before school	101	disease	118
		break	101	fat	118
Unit 6	**Page**	early	102	healthy	118
o'clock	90	on time	102	heart	118
do my homework	91	quickly	102	label	118
evening	91	ready	102	salt	118
get dressed	91	chin	103	sugar	118
get up	91	chop	103	too much	118
go out	91	rich	103	unhealthy	118
go to bed	91	ship	103	pineapple	122
sleep	91	witch	103	watermelon	122
start school	91			avocado	123
stay in bed	91	**Unit 7**	**Page**	chocolate	123
watch	91	apples	112	fabric	123
come back	92	bananas	112	kiwi	123
in the afternoon	92	burgers	112	leaves	123
boring	93	carrots	112	popular	123
finish school	94	cheese	112	tropical	123

Big English Song

From the mountaintops to the bottom of the sea,
From a big blue whale to a baby bumblebee –
If you're big, if you're small, you can have it all
And you can be anything you want to be!

**It's bigger than you. It's bigger than me.
There's so much to do and there's so much to see!
The world is big and beautiful and so are we!
Think big! Dream big! Big English!**

So in every land, from the desert to the sea
We can all join hands and be one big family.
If we love, if we care, we can go anywhere!
The world belongs to everyone; it's ours to share.

**It's bigger than you. It's bigger than me.
There's so much to do and there's so much to see!
The world is big and beautiful and so are we!
Think big! Dream big! Big English!**

**It's bigger than you. It's bigger than me.
There's so much to do and there's so much to see!
The world is big and beautiful and waiting for me.
A one, two, three...
Think big! Dream big! Big English!**

We want to go to the post office.

Is there a post office near here?

I want to buy a book.

Is there a bookshop near here?

My mum wants to eat lunch.

Is there a restaurant near here?

My grandma wants to buy biscuits and milk.

Is there a supermarket near here?

My dad wants to put petrol in the car.

Is there a petrol station near here?

Pearson Education Limited
Edinburgh Gate
Harlow
Essex CM20 2JE
England
and Associated Companies throughout the world.

www.pearsonelt.com/bigenglish

First published 2015
Fourteenth impression 2023

ISBN: 978-1-4479-8913-4

Set in Heinemann Roman
Editorial production and project management S.A.
Printed in Slovakia by Neografia

Acknowledgements

The publisher would like to thank the following for their kind permission to reproduce photographs:

(Key: b-bottom; c-centre; l-left; r-right; t-top)

123RF.com: captblack76 150 (b), Cathy Yeulet 100, Gilberto Mevi 118 (sandwich), Jacek Chabraszewski 28, Jasmin Merdan 27bl, jreika 155r, Lisa Young 12, lsaloni 155l, maxaltamor 42 (a), Nagy-Bagoly Ilona 13/3, Neven Milinković 69 (d), patrickhastings 154l, Pratchaya Leelapatchayanont 139t, romasph 121 (apple), Serhiy Kobyakov 152, tomwang 13/2, viewstock 101t, Virgilijus Norkus 29t; **Alamy Images:** ableimages 94c, 106/4 (centre), Aflo Co. Ltd 150 (a), Alex Segre 58/7, 69 (c), ARGO Images, Art Directors & TRIP 145/5 (2), 160/4 (right), Asia Images Group Pte Ltd 9r, 21br, 27br, 72r, 75bl, 95l, 113/3, 123bl, 140bl, 151, Bert de Ruiter, Blend Images 74/6, 81bl (pilot), Bob Masters 42 (d), BUILT Images 40, Cultura Creative (RF, Danita Delimont 30, David Young-Wolff, Denkou Images 88t, Easy Production 127/1, F1online digitale Bildagentur GmbH 70 (b), Gari Wyn Williams 73/1, Glow Asia RF Stickers (top right), Graham Oliver 58/11, Hemis 64 (d), Ian Dagnall 58/6, imagebroker 68 (b), Jeff Greenberg 4/4, 20/2, 21 (c), Joerg Boethling 46r, KidStock, Martin Wilson 150 (a), myLAM 150 (c), Nikreates 121 (carton of juice), Pawel Libera Images 42 (b), Purepix 31l, Radius Images, simon margetson travel 36br, 52/3 (left), Steve bly 85/3, Ted Foxx 48br, TomBham 58/5, uwe umstatter, VStock 29 (Jim), Zak Waters 86tr; **Corbis:** David Bathgate 15 (d), Jan Haas / dpa 70 (a), Bruce Laurance / Blend Images 1l, Margaret Courtney-Clarke 31r, SUPRI / X00477 / Reuters 47r; **Datacraft Co Ltd:** 70 (c); **DK Images:** Andy Crawford 96 (d), Britta Jaschinski 58/1, 106/1 (left), Cyril Laubscher 140/30 (parrot), Lorenzo Vecchia 122b, 123 (kiwi), Lucy Claxton, Martin Richardson (c) Rough Guides 64 (b), 128/8, 135/2, Max Alexander 73/2, Robert Holmes, Ruth Jenkinson 8/1, Simon Rawles 94b, 106/4 (right), Steve Gorton 16tr, 21 (b), 24 (skateboard), Tim Draper (c) Rough Guides 128/7, Tim Ridley 112/11, Vanessa Davies 4/8, 19/2, William Shaw 112/15, 124/5; **Eyewire:** 20/3, 35/2; **FLPA Images of Nature:** David Hosking 140/29 (d); **Fotolia.com:** abdue 36tr, Alexandra Karamyshev 50cr, Andres Rodriguez 145/5 (1), 160/4 (left), Andrey Bandurenko 37tr, 43/16 (2), apops 80/3, Atiketta Sangasaeng 81bl (table), Berna Şafoğlu 120, clairez 59, Darla Hallmark 43/16 (7), dasharosato 64 (c), dekanaryas 101b, Eric Isselée 135/1, 140/30 (fox), f9photos 96 (a), fotoperle 20/4, 21 (d), George Dolgikh 89/40 (T), Giuseppe Porzani 58/2, 106/1 (centre), goodluz 74/5, 89/2, GoodMood Photo 51/3, 52/4 (centre), Ilike 4/2, Ivonne Wierink 62cr, 66/21 (4), 112/12, 160/1 (centre), Jakub Krechowicz 112/6, jjpixs 13/1, Jose Manuel Gelpi 43/16 (1), Juulijs 16t (centre right), Konovalov Pavel 67/3, krsmanovic 58/3, 106/1 (right), laszlolorik 66/21 (1), Lucky Dragon 32 (a), Lusoimages 50c, Maksim Shebeko 119 (oranges), matka_Wariatka 5t, Michael Ireland 32 (c), Michael Shake 43/16 (3), Monika Wisniewska 86cr, Monkey Business 32 (b), 119 (cookies), moodboard 156/3, Moreno Novello 14 (b), Morphart 43/16 (6), motorlka 112/5, 113 (c), 124/3, 160/1 (right), Natika 118 (crisps), Olga Sapegina 113tr, Pavel Losevsky 58/10, picsfive 118 (chocolate), 121 (chocolate), primopiano 112/13, 121 (burger), r-o-x-o-r 64 (a), Reflekcija 51/1, 52/4 (left), Rob, Robert Wilson 43/16 (5), RT Images 43/16 (8), 50tc, RTimages 20/1, 21 (a), 35/1, 52/2 (left), RusGri 112/14, 124/4, shock 58/8, shutswis 51/4, 52/4 (right), snaptitude Stickers (bottom left), stockphoto-graf 81bl (milk), sumnersgraphicsinc 50tr, sveta 50cl, thepoo 66t, Tom Wang Stickers (bottom right),

tropper2000 124/6, twixx 50tl, Tyler Olson 74/11, 106/2 (right), Václav Hroch 8/2, 13t, vlorzor 143/6, windu 143/3, yanlev 20/7, 52/2 (right); **Getty Images:** Damir Spanic 74/1, David Page Photography 116/2, Diane Collins and Jordan Hollender 4/6, 19/4, 52/1 (right), elvira boix photography 83, Gage 15 (c), JUAN SILVA 48/3, Katy McDonnell 4/3, 8/4, 52/1 (centre), Kazumasa Yanai 37cl, 79/2, Rubberball / Mike Kemp 144; **Glow Images:** Imagemore, Ron Chapple 156/4; **Imagestate Media:** John Foxx Collection 149 (d); **MIXA Co., Ltd:** 149 (c); **Pearson Education:** 20 (background), 24 (basketball), 36-37, 58-59 (background image), 74-75, 79/3; **Pearson Education Ltd:** Studio 8 11br, 18r, 27tr, 43br, 63l, 65br, 66/21 (3), 75br, 81br, 95r, 97br, 119br, 123br, 129br, Sophie Bluy 82, Trevor Clifford 15br, Jules Selmes 4/9, 74/10, Stickers (top left), Naki Kouyioumtzis 58/4, Sozaijiten; **Secretariat of Tourism, Buenos Aires:** Julian W 138l; **Shutterstock.com:** Aaron Amat, Africa Studio 123 (avocado), Alexander Ryabintsev, Alexey Goosev 128/6, 160/2 (centre), Andre Blais 32 (d), Andrjuss 112/9, 121 (cheese), Andy Dean Photography 74/4, Apples Eyes Studio 86tl, artjazz 89/4, AVAVA 98, Blend Images 45bl, 75t, Bruce MacQueen 134/1, Bryan Solomon 118 (cookies), Carlos Neto 128/2, Chris Bence 119 (pizza), Chris Fourie 129cl, Chris Howey 68 (a), Chris Jenner 73/3, Christopher Jones 74/2, 106/2 (left), Christopher Kolaczan 134/4, clawan 154-155 (background), Cora Mueller 20/5, 52/2 (centre), Csaba Peterdi 20/6, 35/4, 156/1, cycreation, davegkugler 128/1, 140/29 (c), 160/2 (right), Dean Bertoncelj 80/2, Diane Garcia 85/2, Diego Cervo 13/4, 91t, Dirk Ercken 136, Dmitriy Shironosov 74/9, Dmitry Naumov 20/8, 156/2, Dudarev Mikhail, Eky Studio 4-5, 20-21, eurobanks 118 (carrots), Evgeny Karandaev, Gemenacom (bike, jacket, skates), Goodluz 80/1, Horiyan 121 (milk), Iakov Filimonov 128/5, Ian Rentoul 139b, idiz 128/3, 137, 160/2 (left), Iriana Shiyan 36bl, 52/3 (centre), irin k, Jacek Chabraszewski 116/3, 127/2, James Steidl 42 (c), Jiri Hera 118 (sweets), John Kasawa 37cr, 51/6, JonMilnes 84, karen roach 73 (ruler), Karkas 44, 62cl, 67/2, 143/2, Kesu 149 (b), Kitch Bain 16tl, kkammphoto008 47l, Kladej, Kokhanchikov 127/4, Kzenon 26tl, Leah-Anne Thompson 145/4 (T), Ledoct 89/3, Lisovskaya Natalia 66/21 (2), Ljupco Smokovski 112/7, 116/4, Lorraine Kourafas 94t, 106/4 (left), Lucky Business 19/3, lynnette 51/2, Mark Bonham 74/3, 106/2 (centre), Matthew Cole 140/30 (snake), mexrix 112/10, 113 (a), Mike Price 135/4, 140/30 (whale), Minerva Studio, Monkey Business Images 4/7, 9l, 18l, 21bl, 26bl, 27bl, 32bl, 32br, 37bl, 37br, 41l, 43cl, 43cr, 50bl, 50br, 65tl, 65tr, 79bl, 79br, 81tr, 85br, 89/1, 91bl, 91br, 107l, 107r, 113/2, 117r, 127/3, 129bl, 133l, 140br, 149bl, 149br, Morgan Lane Photography 4/5, 19/1, MShev 1cr, Natalia Siverina, Nate A 145/4 (B), Naypong 128/11, Nick Berrisford 134/2, Sergey Novikov 1cl, odze 112/3, 113 (b), 121 (strawberries), 160/1 (left), P72 121 (cookies), 124/2, Paleka, Panco, Pavel V Mukhin 143/4, Perig 24 (tree), Peter Wey, photobank.ch 86bl, photocell 112 (placemat), 121 (placemat), PhotoNAN 143/1, ppfoto13 143/5, Presniakov Oleksandr 96 (c), rickyd 128/9, riekephotos 48/2, Rob Marmion 26bc, 35/3, Rohit Seth 29 (Tim), 45c, 79/1, Ronald Summers 24 (football), 62r, 67/1, ruslanchik 119 (salad), Sam Strickler 138r, Sarunyu_foto, Senol Yaman 149 (a), SergiyN 5br, 15bl, 16br, 25r, 48bl, 63r, 81tl, 88b, 97tl, 113/1, 126l, 133r, Serhiy Kobyakov 4/1, 52/1 (left), Shawn Hempel 140/29 (a), sixninepixels 43/16 (4), 51/5, Skazka Grez 118 (apple), Slaven 86cl, Smit, sootra 113 (background), stefanolunardi 1r, Stephanie Frey 48/1, Steve Cukrov 89/40 (B), stockyimages 1c, Stu Porter 128/4, Supertrooper, Tatik22 67/4, Tatuasha, Tatyana Vyc 112/2, 124/1, Tischenko Irina 153, Tomas Loutocky 36tl, 52/3 (right), Tungphoto 37tl, Valentyn Volkov 112/8, 122t, Victor Shova 128/10, Viktar Malyshchyts 62l, 112/1, Visionsi 74/8, Vitaly Korovin 112/4, Vladimir Koletic 74/7, Volodymyr Goinyk 129 (glacier), Warren Goldswain 102, wavebreakmedia 8/3, Willyam Bradberry 134/3, 134-135 (background), worldswildlifewonders 129tr, YapAhock 128/12, 135/3, Yuri Arcurs 29 (Alex), 45br, 79/4, Zadiraka Evgenii 16t (centre left), Peter Zaharov 129cr, Zigroup-Creations 46l, zimmytws 26tr, ZouZou; **SuperStock:** Biosphoto 140/29 (b), Blend Images 5bl, 16bl, 25l, 41r, 72l, 85bl, 97tr, 117l, 126r, Corbis 145/5 (3), 160/4 (centre), DeAgostini 96 (b), Exactostock 26br, Yuri Arcurs Media / SuperFusion 116/1; **www.imagesource.com:** Nigel Riches 29 (Sarah), 45t, photolibrary.com 58/9, 86br

Cover images: Front: Shutterstock.com: Iakov Filimonov l, Dudarev Mikhail c, stockyimages r

All other images © Pearson Education

Every effort has been made to trace the copyright holders and we apologise in advance for any unintentional omissions. We would be pleased to insert the appropriate acknowledgement in any subsequent edition of this publication.

Illustrated by

Robin Boyer, Zaharias Papadopoulos (hyphen), Jose Rubio, Christos Skaltsas (hyphen), Julia Wolf.